MW01228914

The Warnings in Hebrews, Adoption, and Why We Are All Going to Hell

The Warnings in Hebrews, Adoption, and Why We Are All Going to Hell

To Whom Are These Warnings Given?

Daniel R Shannon

MENDING NETS

Published by Mending Nets Ministries, Kaufman TX

www.hopeofglory.net

Copyright © 2022 Daniel R Shannon

All rights reserved. No portion of this book may be reproduced in any form without permission from the publisher, except as permitted by U.S. copyright law. For permissions contact: dannyshannon@disciples.com

Cover by David Smith.

ISBN: 979-8-9860819-1-5

Printed in USA

1st Edition

This work is dedicated to Royce Powell. Brother Royce taught me there are no Bible scholars, only Bible students. Without his upper classman guidance, my studies would not be as far advanced as they are today, and they still have far to go. You will find his influence on many of these pages. He is a dear and precious man who truly loves the Lord.

Table of Contents

Introduction

There have been many books written about the warnings in Hebrews. Some of them are so in-depth that they are overwhelming. Others are fluff and do not cover the important information. Still others miss the point completely.

The goal of this book is to give sufficient information to explain the warnings completely, but not so cumbersome as to become tedious. We want to teach you **_how_** to think, not **_what_** to think.

This study on the warnings in the book of Hebrews originated as a class study on the book of Revelation. The book of Revelation speaks of the wrath of God, so the study referred back to Hebrews and the warnings in that book. This side trip was taken to study the warnings in Hebrews so a better understanding could be reached in regard to the warnings in book of Revelation.

As a foundation for studying the warnings in Hebrews, we had to first undertake a study of salvation, therefore the beginning of the study in Hebrews focuses upon salvation. This study of salvation can also stand on its own.

The translation that we have chosen to use is the New Revised Standard Version (NRSV). Unless otherwise noted, all passages are from the NRSV. Other translations that are used are the Concordant Literal Version (CLV), Young's Literal Translation (YLT), Rotherham's Emphasized Version (REV), and the King James Version (KJV).[1]

---

[1] The YLT is based upon the same text as the KJV, but is a literal translation. The NRSV and KJV both let you know when something is changed in the text: The NRSV uses footnotes and the KJV uses italics. The KJV used footnotes in the older printings, but most modern printings omit translators' footnotes.

All verses in the text are enclosed within brackets [ ]. Notes on the text (alternate meanings of words, expounded meanings of words, underlying words, etc.) are enclosed in brackets within the brackets. [[ ]].[2]

Have a grace day.

---

[2] Example: [1 John 1:9: *If* we confess [present; durative action; continually confess] our sins, he who is faithful and just will forgive us our sins [subjunctive; dependent upon if we confess] and cleanse us from all unrighteousness.]

The Warnings In Hebrews, Adoption, and Why We Are All Going to Hell

The Warnings in Hebrews

In Greek, there are two words for "knowledge": *gnosis* and *epignosis*.

Gnosis means comprehension or an intellectual grasp of something or the content of what is known.

Epignosis means knowledge upon knowledge; a deeper knowledge of that which is being spoken of.

[1 Timothy 2:3-4: This is right and is acceptable in the sight of God our Savior, who desires everyone to be saved and to come to the knowledge [*epignosis*] of the truth.]

[2 Timothy 2:24-25: And the Lord's servant must not be quarrelsome but kindly to everyone, an apt teacher, patient, correcting opponents with gentleness. God may perhaps grant that they will repent and come to know [*epignosis*] the truth...]

[Hebrews 10:26: For if we willfully persist in sin after having received the knowledge [*epignosis*] of the truth, there no longer remains a sacrifice for sins.][3]

[Isaiah 28:9-10: "Whom will he teach knowledge, and to whom will he explain the message? Those who are weaned from milk, those taken from the breast? For it is precept upon precept, precept upon precept, line upon line, line upon line, here a little, there a little."]

---

[3] This passage is not referring to baby believers, this is referring to mature believers who have knowledge upon knowledge.

Why do we need to study?

[Luke 10:41b-42: "Martha, Martha, you are worried and distracted by many things; there is need of only one thing. Mary has chosen the better part, which will not be taken away from her."]

When Jesus went to visit Mary and Martha, Martha went to Jesus and said, "Look: I'm doing all this stuff, and Mary isn't lifting a finger to help me! Make her work!" But Jesus tells us that sitting at his feet and studying is the better part.

Isaiah 28:9-10 is a passage you should print out and post at your desk so you do not forget it. Most doctrine in the Bible is developed a little here and a little there. That is how we choose the better part.

Who in this place is a survivor?

Being called a survivor is not necessarily a compliment.

Survive simply means to continue to live or exist.

What kind of life is that? (A safe one, perhaps.)

Prevail, however, means to overcome, to gain the victory or superiority; to gain the advantage; to have the upper hand; to have the mastery; to win; to triumph; to be victorious; to conquer.

Most people are survivors. There is nothing dishonorable in being a survivor, but merely surviving is a waste of human potential. Why simply survive when you can triumph?

Anyone can become a prevailer but you must know **_how_** to become a prevailer and you must have the discipline to stay the course and avoid mere survival. We all encounter obstacles, but a prevailer comes out on top.

There is a Greek word *nikeo*; it means prevailer or conqueror. That is where the name for the Nike shoes originates. Israel was a prevailer when they followed God. You too can be a prevailer **_if_** you follow God.

That is what these passages are warning about in Hebrews. While we were in our studies in the book of Revelation, we looked briefly at one of the warning passages of Hebrews, and at this point, a study of the warnings in Hebrews will be beneficial to us. Our purpose as we begin this study on the warning passages in Hebrews is to lay a foundation for understanding these warnings, what they mean, and to whom they are written.

What are the five warning passages in Hebrews?

[Hebrews 2:1-5: Therefore we must pay greater attention to what we have heard, so that we do not drift away from it. For if the message declared through angels was valid, and every transgression or disobedience received a just penalty, how can we escape if we neglect so great a salvation? It was declared at first through the Lord, and it was attested to us by those who heard him, while God added his testimony by signs and wonders and various miracles, and by gifts of the Holy Spirit, distributed according to his will. Now God did not subject the coming world, about which we are speaking, to angels.]

[Hebrews 3:7-4:13: Therefore, as the Holy Spirit says, "Today, if you hear his voice, do not harden your hearts as in the rebellion, as on the day of testing in the wilderness, where your ancestors put me to the test, though they had seen my works for forty years. Therefore I was angry with that generation, and I said, 'They always go astray in their hearts, and they have not known my ways.' As in my anger I swore, 'They will not enter my rest.' " Take care, brothers and sisters, that none of you may have an evil, unbelieving heart that turns away from the living God. But exhort one another every day, as long as it is called "today," so that none of you may be hardened by the deceitfulness of sin. For we have become partners of Christ, if only we hold our first confidence firm to the end. As it is said, "Today, if you hear his voice, do not harden your hearts as in the rebellion."

Now who were they who heard and yet were rebellious? Was it not all those who left Egypt under the leadership of Moses? But with whom was he angry forty years? Was it not those who sinned, whose bodies fell in the wilderness? And to whom did he swear that they would not enter his rest, if not to those who were disobedient? So we see that they were unable to enter because of unbelief.

Therefore, while the promise of entering his rest is still open, let us take care that none of you should seem to have failed to reach it. For indeed the good news came to us just as to them; but the message they heard did not benefit them, because they were not united by faith with those who listened. For we who have believed enter that rest, just as God has said, "As in my anger I swore, 'They shall not enter my rest,' " though his works were finished at the foundation of the world. For in one place it speaks about the seventh day as follows, "And God rested on the seventh day from all his works." And again in this place it says, "They shall not enter my rest." Since therefore it remains open for some to enter it, and those who formerly received the good news failed

to enter because of disobedience, again he sets a certain day—
"today"—saying through David much later, in the words already
quoted, "Today, if you hear his voice, do not harden your hearts."

For if Joshua had given them rest, God would not speak later
about another day. So then, a sabbath rest still remains for the
people of God; for those who enter God's rest also cease from
their labors as God did from his. Let us therefore make every
effort to enter that rest, so that no one may fall through such
disobedience as theirs.

Indeed, the word of God is living and active, sharper than any
two-edged sword, piercing until it divides soul from spirit, joints
from marrow; it is able to judge the thoughts and intentions[4] of
the heart. And before him no creature is hidden, but all are naked
and laid bare to the eyes of the one to whom we must render an
account.]

[Hebrews 6:4-8: For it is impossible to restore again to
repentance those who have once been enlightened, and have
tasted the heavenly gift, and have shared in the Holy Spirit, and
have tasted the goodness of the word of God and the powers of
the age to come, and then have fallen away, since on their own
they are crucifying again the Son of God and are holding him up
to contempt. Ground that drinks up the rain falling on it
repeatedly, and that produces a crop useful to those for whom it
is cultivated, receives a blessing from God. But if it produces
thorns and thistles, it is worthless and on the verge of being
cursed; its end is to be burned over.]

---

[4] You will hear me repeat this quite often, but while God may know the
intentions of the heart, it is the direction, not the intention, that determines the
destination. We all know which road is paved with good intentions.

[Hebrews 10:26-39: For if we willfully persist in sin after having received the knowledge of the truth, there no longer remains a sacrifice for sins, but a fearful prospect of judgment, and a fury of fire that will consume the adversaries. Anyone who has violated the law of Moses dies without mercy "on the testimony of two or three witnesses." How much worse punishment do you think will be deserved by those who have spurned the Son of God, profaned the blood of the covenant by which they were sanctified, and outraged the Spirit of grace? For we know the one who said, "Vengeance is mine, I will repay." And again, "The Lord will judge his people." It is a fearful thing to fall into the hands of the living God.

But recall those earlier days when, after you had been enlightened, you endured a hard struggle with sufferings, sometimes being publicly exposed to abuse and persecution, and sometimes being partners with those so treated. For you had compassion for those who were in prison, and you cheerfully accepted the plundering of your possessions, knowing that you yourselves possessed something better and more lasting. Do not, therefore, abandon that confidence of yours; it brings a great reward. For you need endurance, so that when you have done the will of God, you may receive what was promised.

For yet "in a very little while, the one who is coming will come and will not delay; but my righteous one will live by faith. My soul takes no pleasure in anyone who shrinks back." But we are not among those who shrink back and so are lost, but among those who have faith and so are saved.]

[Hebrews 12:25-29: See that you do not refuse the one who is speaking; for if they did not escape when they refused the one who warned them on earth, how much less will we escape if we reject the one who warns from heaven! At that time his voice shook the earth; but now he has promised, "Yet once more I will shake not only the earth but also the heaven." This phrase, "Yet once more," indicates the removal of what is shaken—that is, created things—so that what cannot be shaken may remain. Therefore, since we are receiving a kingdom that cannot be shaken, let us give thanks, by which we offer to God an acceptable worship with reverence and awe; for indeed our God is a consuming fire.]

To whom are these warnings written?

[Hebrews 13:22: I appeal to you, brothers and sisters [brethren], bear with my word of exhortation, for I have written to you briefly.]

Who are brothers and sisters?

[Matthew 12:50: For whoever does the will of my Father in heaven is my brother and sister and mother.]

What is the will of the Father?

[John 6:29: Jesus answered them, "This is the work of God, that you believe in him whom he has sent."]

In this passage, the word "believe" is present, active, and is synonymous with faith; it is saying, "be faithful". The work of God is to be faithful; in order to be faithful, you must know how to be faithful, and you can know how to be faithful by study and building line upon line.

11

These warnings are written to all the readers, not just a part of them; those who are faithful. These warnings are written to those who would be prevailers and conquerors, and not merely survivors. A prize that is worth winning has to be **_won_**!

How much value is placed upon a first place trophy if every participant gets a first place trophy? That is merely a participation trophy. There is nothing dishonorable in a participation trophy, but neither is it worth very much.

A central theme of the Bible centers on salvation and eternal life, and Hebrews is certainly no exception. On the surface, it seems like a simple subject, but is it simple?

Salvation is a multi-faceted truth that glorifies God. It is presented in various ways, but all the ways surround a three-fold aspect of salvation that applies to a trichotomous (three-part) being. Salvation has a past sense, present sense, and a future sense that corresponds to the spirit, soul, and body.[5]

[1 Thessalonians 5:23: May the God of peace himself sanctify you entirely; and may your spirit **_and_** soul **_and_** body be kept sound [complete] and blameless at the coming of our Lord Jesus Christ.]

There is the past aspect of salvation (spirit; redemption[6]), the present aspect (soul; sanctification), and the future aspect (body;

---

[5] This is what distinguishes man from the other animals. God breathed the spirit into man (body), and man became a living soul. Genesis 1 tells us that animals have a sprit and soul, but only the spirit of man is from God.

[6] There is also a past aspect of justification. We have been justified, but we are also working that we may one day be justified. The past tense gave us a clean slate, but our present actions affect our future justification, so that we may one

glorification[7]). Those who have been born from above into the family of God have been saved, are obtaining salvation, and await salvation. From the time I was a child, I have heard more than one teacher put it as, "I am saved, I am being saved, and I will be saved".

Because there is more than one aspect of salvation, we must determine the context of a passage on salvation or we will have contradictions, enigmas, and conundrums. If the proper context is determined, a correct (and simple) interpretation will be achieved. Any text without a context is a pretext. If we study, we can determine the proper context.

[1 Timothy 2:15: Yet she will be saved through childbearing, provided they continue in faith and love and holiness, with modesty.]

[Matthew 8:25: And they went and woke him up, saying, "Lord, save us! We are perishing!"]

These two verses show that when the Bible is speaking about the word "saved", it is not always referring to the same thing.

Salvation tends to be comparative. In other words, comparing or contrasting one state with another. Hence, the Philippian jailor wanted to know how to be saved as opposed to unsaved (the event that puts us into the family; born from above). The salvation of the soul is present tense and is contrasted with forfeiting our inheritance or our future ruling and reigning in the coming

---

day hear, "Well done". I have heard the future aspect stated, "To justify the justified".

[7] This is the reference for the hope of glory in Colossians 1:27. This has to do with our future justification, which is based upon our present actions.

Kingdom. Saved out of a pit as contrasted to being in the pit. The word "salvation" is not an absolute.

The failure to make this distinction between the uses of the word "salvation" has led to schisms within the church and centuries of arguments about once-saved-always-saved or not. One side looks at certain passages while ignoring others, while the other side ignores the first passages and looks only at the others, while many who are in neither camp simply throw their hands up in the air and say it does not matter just so long as we believe **_something_**.

If we try to apply only one meaning to the word "salvation", we will have to ignore many (or most) of the passages about salvation, unless we are willing to accept contradictions. If one thinks the Bible contains contradictions, he may as well discard it; what good is it if it is faulty?

The Bible is not faulty; there are **_no_** contradictions! There may be things we do not understand and they may seem like contradictions, but there are no contradictions.

The Bible uses at least eight different meanings for the word "salvation", most of which have to do with healing, national, personal, or spiritual salvation. Only a small portion of the time is it reference to the final destiny of the unsaved. In Psalm 78:22, "God's saving power" has to do with his ability to feed them and give them water in the wilderness, and obviously had nothing to do with whether or not they were going to heaven.

Salvation has distinct differences and meanings and creates a condition of duality.

There are many distinctions made throughout the Bible, and one of those is a distinction made between the death of Jesus on the cross and the shedding of his blood.

[2 Corinthians 5:14-15: For the love of Christ urges us on, because we are convinced that one has died for all; therefore all have died. And he died for all, so that those who live might live no longer for themselves, but for him who died and was raised for them.]

[Mark 14:24: He said to them, "This is my blood of the covenant, which is poured out for many.]

[Hebrews 13:20-21: Now may the God of peace, who brought back from the dead our Lord Jesus, the great shepherd of the sheep, by the blood of the eternal covenant, make you complete in everything good so that you may do his will, working among us that which is pleasing in his sight, through Jesus Christ, to whom be the glory forever and ever. Amen.]

"What must I do to be saved?" There is only one place in the Bible where this question is both asked and answered.

[Acts 16:30-31: Then he brought them outside and said, "Sirs, what must I do to be saved?" They answered, "Believe on the Lord Jesus, and you will be saved, you and your household."]

In this passage, "believe" is an aorist, active, imperative verb. The aorist tense shows an event. It is like squeezing the trigger of a gun. You cannot unsqueeze the trigger. By the same token, you can stop believing in something but you cannot undo the fact that you believed.

15

It is a command that requires the individual to believe and it is an event, not a process. This does not simply mean to believe that he exists. It means to accept the need for a savior, and believe in Jesus as that savior.

Believe and you will be saved. The result of this event is that the individual will be saved, and the same applies to those in his house. It does not say that he "might be saved if he continues in good works", or anything else. It simply says, "Believe (event) and you **will be** (not "may be") saved". Period. There is **no** other way to translate this passage, and no other way it can be properly interpreted. Neither is there a text, nor even a manuscript, of which I am aware, that has anything different, except some texts add the word "Christ", after "Jesus".

Yet in other places we are told to strive for salvation or to hold onto salvation. Is this a contradiction?

What is the salvation in this passage in Acts?

Some refer to this salvation, which is irrevocable, as fire insurance. It is a get out of hell free card. My Dad hates it when I use this expression, but it is true: This is the way many use this gift.

Do not make the mistake that many make by teaching this as a license to sin. Far from it! As we shall see, although this salvation cannot be forfeited, the believer is accountable. Both the event and the process are referred to as "salvation". The process (salvation in the present tense) has to do with one's inheritance, not with whether one is in the family or not.

Settling for this salvation in Acts 16 alone is for survivors, not prevailers. This common salvation is what is being spoken of in John 3:3.

[John 3:1-3: Now there was a Pharisee named Nicodemus, a leader of the Jews. He came to Jesus by night and said to him, "Rabbi, we know that you are a teacher who has come from God; for no one can do these signs that you do apart from the presence of God." Jesus answered him, "Very truly, I tell you, no one can see the kingdom of God without being born from above."][8]

Does it take any works on the baby's part to be born? No, it just simply has to be his time. And when it is his time, he will be quite insistent!

Unless one is born from above, he cannot _see_ the Kingdom. This is talking about the same thing that Acts 16:30-31 is speaking of. The things of God are not apparent to the natural man; he must be born from above in order to begin to understand the things of God.

Nicodemus then asks, "How can we climb back in the womb and be born again?"

[John 3:5: Jesus answered, "Very truly, I tell you, no one can enter the kingdom of God without being born of water and Spirit.][9]

---

[8] Some translations have "born again" in this verse, but it is properly "born from above". Being born from above is the first birth for a believer. There is nothing for the believer to do but believe and he is in the family of God. This word "above" in "born from above" is the same word that is used in John 3:31 that says, "He that is from above is over all…"

[9] This verse presents the same idea as that presented in 1 Peter, which is born again, as opposed to born from above. It involves works. Some of the oldest

This idea involves works and it is talking about an ***entrance*** into the Kingdom.

An entrance is more than simply seeing the Kingdom. To have an entrance means to be a partaker of or to go in and possess the land as the Israelites possessed Canaan.

There are two lands of promise given to Abraham; a type of the earthly seed and the heavenly seed. The first land of promise is based on nothing other than being in the family. The first land of promise is found in Genesis 15:18, which promises the land from the Nile to the Euphrates. Before the children of Israel left Egypt, they were already there! But the land flowing with milk and honey was promised based upon faithful service and that land of promise followed baptism in the Red Sea and a spirit-filled life wandering through the desert. One Promised Land is within the other. Only those who were in the land from the Nile to the Euphrates could enter into the land flowing with milk and honey but not everyone in that land of promise entered the land flowing with milk and honey.

Abraham had three seeds: The first two are collective, one being as the sands on the seashore and the other as the stars in heaven. (Interestingly, man at that time thought there were only a few thousand stars, because that is all that were visible. However, we now know, as has been revealed to us through telescopes, that there are untold billions of stars.) The third seed is singular, and that seed is Jesus.

---

manuscripts say, "no one can enter the Kingdom without being born ***again*** of water and spirit."

[Deuteronomy 34:1: Then Moses went up from the plains of Moab to Mount Nebo, to the top of Pisgah, which is opposite Jericho, and the LORD showed him the whole land…]

Here, the Lord and Moses are together in the plains of Moab, on the mountain of Nebo, and Moses is looking across the Jordan and he is seeing Jericho. Moses was in the middle of the land and he had a clear perspective all the way to the north and to the south. The Lord showed him all the land of Gilead unto Dan; and all of Naphtali and the land of Ephraim and all the land of Manasseh and all the land of Judah unto the utmost sea (the Mediterranean Sea), and unto the south and all of the plain and valley of Jericho, and the City of Palm Trees unto Zoar.

The Lord said to Moses, "This is the Land". "Moses, I am showing you the land." Moses is seeing the land that God was showing to him.

[Deuteronomy 34:4-5: The LORD said to him, "This is the land of which I swore to Abraham, to Isaac, and to Jacob, saying, 'I will give it to your descendants' [your seed]; I have let you see it with your eyes, but you shall not cross over there." Then Moses, the servant of the LORD, died there in the land of Moab, at the LORD's command.]

Moses _saw_, but he could not _enter_ in. He was in the land of promise (the Nile to the Euphrates) but he could not enter into the land flowing with milk and honey, which was the better inheritance that was promised based upon faithfulness.

The better inheritance is representative of the heavenly inheritance, as opposed to the earthly inheritance. Throughout the Bible, there are two inheritances presented: Birth-inheritance and

19

reward-inheritance. This remains consistent throughout the Scriptures.

The land of Canaan is a type or a picture of the Kingdom of the Heavens, or the Kingdom of God. The Bible teaches in John chapter 1:17 that, "The law indeed was given through Moses; grace and truth came through Jesus Christ." The law will bring us up to the Jordan River to give us a view of the land that God promised to Abraham, Isaac and Jacob.

He did not promise the better land to Moses. Is that not interesting? "I have promised this to Abraham, Isaac and Jacob and to their seed, but not to you, Moses."

The thing about the Lord is this; he does not simply have a bunch of brochures printed up by AAA to describe the land, although, that is sort of what we have today in the Bible. In the days of Moses spies were sent out to check out Kadesh Barnea and come back and give a report. They came back and gave reports and bring back samples.

[Numbers 13:25-27: At the end of forty days they returned from spying out the land. And they came to Moses and Aaron and to all the congregation of the Israelites in the wilderness of Paran, at Kadesh; they brought back word to them and to all the congregation, and showed them the fruit of the land. And they told him, "We came to the land to which you sent us; it flows with milk and honey, and this is its fruit."]

The children of Israel did not have enough faith to simply believe God when he told them about the land. They wanted to see it with their own eyes, instead of walking by faith. We see that in the Church today with people wanting signs instead of walking by faith, and just like the children of Israel, the church still are not faithful, even with knowledge.

The Israelites had direct knowledge of the land; the spies had to carry a cluster of grapes between two men upon a staff, and they brought some pomegranates and some figs. Can you imagine carrying a cluster of grapes that takes two men to carry? I bet they were good, too. God does not give us bad fruit.

We have the brochures (in the Bible), but the spies were able to go over and see it with their own eyes, and they were able to say, "It's just like the Lord said it was". The Lord let them have some big, tasty grapes, some pomegranates, and some figs, and they were good. Yet, after everything they had been shown, the first response by the masses was, "Run away!"

I want us to look at a passage in a book that is often neglected. If you ever want to find it, it is over past 2 Chronicles, not too much before you get to Job. If you find yourself in Esther's house, turn one door to the left.

[Nehemiah 9:16-17: "But they and our ancestors acted presumptuously and stiffened their necks and did not obey your commandments; they refused to obey, and were not mindful of the wonders that you performed among them; but they stiffened their necks and determined to return to their slavery in Egypt. But you are a God ready to forgive, gracious and merciful, slow to anger and abounding in steadfast love, and you did not forsake them.]

This is referring to the nation of Israel at the time of the events that took place at Kadesh Barnea, which was about two years into their journey. They had some fried apple pies, and some pomegranate jam, and some Fig Newtons; they ate that fruit. Yet it tells us here that they acted presumptuously, they stiffened their necks, they hardened their hearts, they harkened not, they refused to obey, they did not want to think about it, and neither were they mindful of the wonders. They rebelled and they wanted to go back to easy and simple slavery in Egypt.

They were already in the land of promise, but the children of Israel wanted to turn back from the blessings the Lord had in store for them and return to the pleasures of their former lives.

Do you want to turn back to the pleasures of your life from before you turned your life over to Jesus or do you want to persevere to the land flowing with milk and honey?

You probably did not feel guilty about your behavior back then, did you? I know that I did not. We did not know better. Sometimes it is easier to turn back. Being obedient to God is sometimes hard, and at other times, it is **_very_** hard. The Lord never said it would be easy.

There are Christians like that today; they want to turn back. You start talking about the coming Kingdom and ruling and reigning, and all the hardships involved and being faithful and behaving yourself like you should, and they want to go back to bondage. They do not want to cross over the Jordan River. They want to take the easy way and they do not care if they come up short. Faithfulness is hard! If it were easy, everyone would be faithful.

The Lord was not unkind to the children of Israel when they wanted to stop short of the Jordan River. They had been eating manna for a long time. God did not tell them, "When you cross over the Jordan and start fighting, I'm going to stop feeding you and your shoes will wear out and your clothes will wear out and your feet might even swell; I'm finished watching over you!" He did not tell them that. What did he do? He gave them encouragement!

That is what we need to be doing today. If you are in the family of God, you can see what He has prepared for us. We need to be concentrating on that and thinking about that.

We do not want to stop short of the Jordan River. We do not simply want to see the Kingdom. We want to enter in; we want to be partakers of that Kingdom; we want to go in and possess the land; we want to be partners.

[John 3:5: Jesus answered, "Very truly, I tell you, no one can enter the kingdom of God without being born [out] of water and Spirit.]

In this verse, we have the word "water" and the word "spirit"; this is a compound prepositional phrase. A preposition is a word that is used with a noun or pronoun to make it so that it can be used as an adjective or adverb. Both the water and spirit are covered by one preposition "of", so the words "water" and "spirit" can both be taken literally, or can both be used figuratively; not one of each; you may not mix and match.

Unless a person is born [again] out of water and out of spirit, he cannot **_enter_** into the Kingdom of God.

There are some who believe this is speaking of baptism and the Holy Spirit, but I do not believe that is correct, although it is something that I have taught in the past. There is no definite article with the word "spirit".

[John 3:6: What is born of the flesh is flesh, and what is born of the Spirit is spirit.]

Verse 6 is explaining what verse 5 is teaching, verse 6 says, "That which is born of flesh is flesh and that which is born of the Spirit is spirit."

There are those that teach that if you are not baptized, you are not saved. That's called baptismal regeneration. Acts 16:31 refutes that. Or at least it forces us to look at what the word "saved" means.

John 3:5 is dealing with an entrance; a full allotment. There is a big difference between seeing and entering, as we saw in the example of Moses. There are those who are qualified to enter the game and those who can simply see the game.

Anyone with a ticket can see the game, but you have to qualify to enter the game.

My son and I like to go to motorcycle races. If someone were to give you a ticket, you could go too. No qualifications, you would simply say, "I have a ticket". However, if you wanted to enter the race, you would have to qualify, and that is very difficult. You have to pass a knowledge test of the rules, a technical test to show your bike is safe, and a performance test. Once you do that, you can enter the race, but you are also continuously monitored to make sure you remain qualified. And not everyone who enters the race comes in first place. Not everyone is honored equally. Not everyone who enters even finishes; not everyone comes in second or third. Some crash out. Some are even caught cheating or not acting appropriately and are thrown out and dishonored.

Anyone with a ticket can see the race, and Jesus has provided tickets to anyone who wants one, free of charge to the receiver, with the price paid in full by his sacrifice upon the cross. However, you have to **_work_** if you want to enter the race and win the prize. Let us esteem the rewards that he has promised for faithful service!

When speaking about law and grace, people often say, quite emphatically, "I'm not under the law! I'm under grace!" And that **_is_** what it says in Romans 6:14.

[Romans 6:14: For sin will have no dominion over you, since you are not under law but under grace.]

I have read this passage many times, and I have read through the Bible several times in several different translations, and they all say we are not under the law. But not a single one of them says we are **_above_** the law. Why are we not above the law? **_Because_** we are under grace. To be obedient, we have to abide by the law that God has given us. We must be faithful, not for common salvation, but for obedience. You cannot be lawless and remain under grace.

How can we be obedient? All our righteousnesses are as filthy rags, we are told in Isaiah 64:6.

[Hebrews 12:28: Therefore, since we are receiving a kingdom that cannot be shaken, let us ~~give thanks~~ have grace[10], by which we offer to God an acceptable worship [divine service; serve him acceptably] with reverence and awe]

---

[10] Almost every translation has "have grace" here. It is present, active, and should be "let us keep having grace".

We need grace in order to not only serve God, but to serve God acceptably. "But I am too weak to serve God!" you might say. God's grace is the power of Christ!

[2 Corinthians 12:9a: but he said to me, "My grace is sufficient for you, for power is made perfect in weakness."]

Grace is not unmerited favor, as many teach; grace is the power of Christ! You are too weak to serve God under your own power, but through the power of Christ, you have the power of grace in order to serve acceptably.

How do we obtain this grace?

[Romans 5:1-2: Therefore, since we are justified by faith, we [let us] have peace with God through our Lord Jesus Christ, through whom we have obtained access [by faith] to this grace in which we stand; and we [let us] boast in our hope of sharing the glory of God.]

To be obedient, we have to abide by the law that God has given us.

However, the law is not enough. The blessings under grace are much greater than the blessings under law. Under the law, they did have a blessing from God. Half the tribe of Manasseh, Reuben, and Gad, and even the descendants of Esau had a portion given to them in the land. But their portions were not the best part. Their portions were where the law was given. Their portions were in the wilderness.

That is how the law operates. Did your Granny ever send you out to get a hickory stick? Mine did.[11] The law is living under the hickory stick. When you graduate from the hickory stick to grace, how much better is that? Discipline and the law says we can cross the Jordan on dry ground to get to the land flowing with milk and honey, but when we get there, we have to *take* it! We have to possess the land by defeating our enemies. That is why we have spiritual warfare today. It is not simply to give us something to do from one Sunday to the next.

If we do not fight a good fight, we will not enter into (possess) our inheritance. We may get something good, but we will come up short. Reuben, Manasseh and Gad had to fight so their brothers could enter in, but they did not get the same blessings that their brothers got. Sometimes, God's children have to fight "just because". That may sound terrible, but that is just the way it is. Not all blessings are the same for all God's children.

If you live under the law, law has dominion over you. If you serve sin, you will perish in the wilderness just as Moses did, along with all those who were 20 years and older when they left Egypt.

If grace reigns, you are neither under the law nor above the law.

However, grace might not reign in your life. If you want grace to reign, it takes obedience.

[Romans 5:21a: so that, just as sin exercised dominion in death, so grace might also exercise dominion through justification [righteousness]]

---

[11] And it better not be the smallest one on the tree or *she* would go out and get one and it would be much worse.

[Luke 1:6: Both of them [Zechariah and Elizabeth] were righteous before God, living blamelessly [walking] according to all the commandments and regulations of the Lord.]

[1 Timothy 1:8-11: Now we know that the law is good, if one uses it legitimately. This means understanding that the law is laid down not for the innocent but for the lawless and disobedient, for the godless and sinful, for the unholy and profane, for those who kill their father or mother, for murderers, fornicators, sodomites, slave traders, liars, perjurers, and whatever else is contrary to the sound teaching that conforms to the glorious gospel of the blessed God, which he entrusted to me.]

The righteous are those who are being obedient, and those who are being obedient are the ones who are living under grace. The law was not written for those who are obedient.

Does everyone here carry a big book of traffic laws with you in your car? As you approach a stop sign, do you pull out that book, turn to the correct page, and see what you are supposed to do or do you simply stop? If you are obedient, you simply stop. The law is not written for the obedient.

The law was written for a long list of people in this passage we just read. The law was written so we may have an understanding of sin. If you put yourself under the law, sin is in dominion of your life, you will dwell upon your sin, and you are a servant of sin. We need to simply behave ourselves and serve grace!

Many teach that Ishmael was disinherited. Isaac and Ishmael are both heirs, but they were not joint heirs; their inheritances were not equal. It is interesting to see what Ishmael received as an inheritance.

28

[Genesis 21:13-14: As for the son of the slave woman, I will make a nation of him also, because he is your offspring [your seed]." So Abraham rose early in the morning, and took bread and a skin of water, and gave it to Hagar, putting it on her shoulder, along with the child, and sent her away. And she departed, and wandered about in the wilderness of Beer-sheba.]

Ishmael's inheritance was a loaf of bread and a jug of water. We know that was enough because God promised it, but there is no comparison between that and what Isaac received as an inheritance!

[Genesis 25:5: Abraham gave all he had to Isaac.]

If you want to live under the law, you are a survivor and you will be satisfied with a little food and a little water; just enough to get by.

Never forget, however, that Ishmael received an inheritance! The Lord had plans for him. He had 12 sons just as Jacob did.

Both Isaac and Ishmael received an inheritance from Abraham, but compare bread and water to that which Isaac received: Isaac's inheritance under grace was far superior to the one Ishmael received under the law. What did Abraham have? He had camels, sheep, cattle, gold, silver, servants, BMWs, a Mercedes, and an RV.

[1 Corinthians 2:9: But, as it is written, "What no eye has seen, nor ear heard, nor the human heart conceived, what God has prepared for those who love him"]

29

These things are given to us as types. Compare the inheritance of Ishmael to Isaac. Which is better? Compare that type to the inheritance of seeing the Kingdom versus entering the Kingdom. Why would anyone choose anything less than the blessings of the inheritance of the Kingdom of the Heavens through grace? Seeing the Kingdom is better than missing out altogether, but an entrance – a full allotment – is much better.

[Hebrews 4:8-11: For if Joshua had given them rest, God would not speak later about another day. So then, a sabbath rest still remains for the people of God; for those who enter God's rest also cease from their labors as God did from his. Let us therefore make every effort to enter that rest, so that no one may fall through such disobedience as theirs.]

"Let us therefore make every effort to enter that rest." Let us labor. This is talking about works and a reward for those labors. We have to fight a good warfare. We cannot settle for being survivors, we must be prevailers. We must be victorious! We have to earn the prize. We must not let our enemies defeat us.

[2 Peter 1:10-11: Therefore, brothers and sisters, be all the more eager to confirm your call and election, for if you do this, you will never stumble. For in this way, entry into the eternal kingdom of our Lord and Savior Jesus Christ will be richly provided for you.]

If you do these things, you will have an abundant entrance; the entrance will be richly provided for you. If we do what things?

[2 Peter 1:5-9: For this very reason, you must make every effort to support your faith with goodness, and goodness with knowledge, and knowledge with self-control, and self-control with endurance, and endurance with godliness, and godliness with ~~mutual~~ [brotherly] affection, and ~~mutual~~ [brotherly] affection with love. For if these things are yours and are increasing among you, they keep you from being ineffective and unfruitful in the knowledge of our Lord Jesus Christ. For anyone who lacks these things is nearsighted and blind, and is forgetful of the cleansing of past sins.]

To your faith, you have to add goodness. This is moral excellence. You have to start out with faith and add to it. Goodness means behaving yourself. It means obedience. It means doing the things that God has commanded.

To goodness you must add knowledge. This is the word *gnosis*. This is simple comprehension or an intellectual grasp. You must have knowledge of the Word of God in order to properly arm yourself for spiritual warfare. Proper preparation prevents poor performance.

To knowledge, you must add self-control. You must control your flesh. You must keep your passions and desires in check. The world teaches, "If it feels good, do it". The world teaches that you cannot help the way you behave; everything is an illness or an addiction, but this is simply an excuse. The world is at enmity with God and with godliness. For an abundant entrance, you need to control yourself.

To self-control, you must add endurance or patience. If you endure, you will have a better inheritance. You might have to suffer in order to add endurance. Suffering produces endurance.

Dr. Ironside once related a story in which a woman came up to him and asked him to pray for her because she needed patience.

31

So, he grabbed her hands, bowed his head and said, "Oh, Lord, please bring great tribulation upon this fine woman!" She said, "No, no! I asked for patience!" To which he replied, "Don't you know that Romans 5:3 tells us that 'tribulation worketh patience'?"

To endurance, add godliness. This is devoutness. Worship rightly directed. The word "worship" in English means "worth-ship" or reverence paid to worth, whether of God or man.

[1 Timothy 3:14-16: I hope to come to you soon, but I am writing these instructions to you so that, if I am delayed, you may know how one ought to behave in the household of God, which is the church of the living God, the pillar and bulwark of the truth. Without any doubt, the mystery[12] of our religion [godliness][13] is great: He [which] was revealed in flesh, Vindicated [justified] in spirit, seen by angels, proclaimed among Gentiles, believed in throughout the world, taken up in glory.]

The connection of thought with the mystery of godliness is tied back to "the truth" in verse 15. "The mystery of godliness" is a paraphrase of "the truth". The church is the pillar and stay of the truth and the truth constitutes the mystery of godliness.

The contents of the truth is Christ, as revealed in the gospel as the savior from ungodliness, and he sets the norm for godliness.

---

[12] A mystery is something that has been hidden and is now revealed. This mystery was hidden and then revealed in the work and person of Jesus the Christ. It is concealed from human wisdom but is apprehended by faith in the revelation of God through the Christ.

[13] This word is used in a backhanded way to refer to religion, but it specifically has to do with godliness or piety.

[John 14:6: Jesus said to him, "I am the way, and the truth, and the life. No one comes to the Father except through me.]

The mystery of godliness is the substance of piety, which is the mystery of faith. Faith is a noun that results in a godly lifestyle, and faith is a mystery that must be revealed to each individual.

[1 Timothy 3:9: they [deacons] must hold fast to the mystery of the faith with a clear conscience.]

Deacons are servants, and to be a good servant, one must hold fast with a clear conscience. Why is it important to be a good servant? Matthew 20:26b-27: but whoever wishes to be great among you must be your servant, and whoever wishes to be first among you must be your slave.

Back in 2 Peter 1: To godliness, add brotherly affection.

There are three words in Greek for "love". The first one is "*eros*" which is romantic or physical love. It is not used in the Bible.

The second word is "*phileo*", which means brotherly love. It is where we get the name of the city of Philadelphia and why its nickname is "the city of brotherly love." That is the word that is used here: "*Philadelphian*".

To brotherly affection, add love. This is the third word for "love", which is *Agape*. This is love by deliberate choice. *Agape* is more extensive in its objects and acts.[14]

---

[14] There is also a fourth word that can be translated as "love", and that is *storge*, which is a natural affection, such as that between parents and children. This word, as with *eros*, is absent in the Bible.

[2 Peter 1:10b: …for if you do this, you will never stumble.]

This word "never" is "*ou mE*": This is a double negative. In the Greek, the double negative is an emphatic **_no_**.

Do these things and you will not fall. You **_will not_** fail. You will prevail! If you do not fall, an abundant or rich entrance will be yours in the coming Kingdom and glory.

[John 3:5b: no one can enter the kingdom of God without being born [out] of water and Spirit.]

This is talking about entering the Kingdom, and a man who is not born of water and spirit cannot enter into the Kingdom. This is talking about law and grace; both apply. We need to behave **_and_** we need to trust Him. We **_can_** trust Him; He has shown us that.

Fellowship will help us in our walk.

[1 John 1:1-4: We declare to you what was from the beginning, what we have heard, what we have seen with our eyes, what we have looked at and touched with our hands, concerning the word of life—this life was revealed, and we have seen it and testify to it, and declare to you the eternal life that was with the Father and was revealed to us—we declare to you what we have seen and heard **_so that you also may have fellowship with us; and truly our fellowship is with the Father and with his Son Jesus Christ_**. We are writing these things so that our [your] joy may be complete.]

There are some essential things we need if we are to have real fellowship. What John is doing in these first three verses is laying out that **_doctrine_** is needed for real fellowship. Sound doctrine is essential in fellowship.

Sound doctrine keeps you from wavering; it keeps you from being tossed to and fro and blown about by every wind of doctrine; it keeps you from being deceived by the sleight of men and cunning craftiness.

[Ephesians 4:14: We must no longer be children, tossed to and fro and blown about by every wind of doctrine, by people's trickery, by their craftiness in deceitful scheming.]

[James 1:6-8: But ask in faith, never doubting[15], for the one who doubts is like a wave of the sea, driven and tossed by the wind. for the doubter, being double-minded and unstable in every way, must not expect to receive anything from the Lord.]

[Acts 2:32; 42: This Jesus God raised up, and of that all of us are witnesses… They [those who were added by Peter's preaching] devoted themselves to the apostles' **_teaching_** [doctrine] and **_fellowship_**, to the **_breaking of bread_** and **_the prayers_**.]

They devoted themselves (they were steadfast; they continued; the verb is "persevering", present, active; they were prevailers) to four things: The doctrine of the apostles, fellowship, the breaking of bread, and prayers. There is a word order in this list. Doctrine comes first. Doctrine is followed by fellowship, and fellowship precedes the breaking of bread and prayers.

Word order is important. The order of these four things is important. Doctrine comes first, followed closely by fellowship.

---

[15] This is not the same thing as complete unbelief, but more of a wavering between faith and unbelief that leans more toward the unbelief than faith.

The verse is divided into two parts grammatically, with doctrine and fellowship included together with each other first, and then breaking of bread and the prayers connected together with each other.

Fellowship is essential to living a Christian life; it is essential to walk your walk in obedience. Without sound doctrine, you cannot have fellowship. If you do not have fellowship, you isolate yourself. If you isolate yourself, you are in danger of making shipwreck of the faith. (In this day and age, it's easier than in the past to fellowship when you are not together in person, but being together is the better way.)

[Revelation 3:20: Listen! I am standing [present tense] at the door, knocking [present tense]; *if* you hear my voice and open the door, I will come in to you and eat with you, and you with me.]

This is not talking about simply being born from above, this is talking about fellowship! Jesus has been standing at the door and is knocking on the door of your heart, not in order that you can be born from above, but in order to have fellowship. This message is to a church that has lost their vision, and there is no such thing as an unsaved church!

There is only one way to have fellowship with the Lord: Through the Word of God. The church at Laodicea, to whom this passage was written, was simply lukewarm; they were self-sufficient and in need of nothing. This church was in such a spiritual condition that the Lord could not get in and have any meaningful fellowship with them.

In Revelation 3:20, the invitation to have fellowship with him is being extended to anyone who hears him knocking and responds. Fellowship has to do with eating and talking about things of common interest. Do you have anyone with whom you fellowship? What do you do with that person? You talk and walk and enjoy each other's company!

Notice that it says, "I will come in to you and eat with you". If he is going to come in and eat with you (or with the church at Laodicea), there has to be preparation on the other side of that door! Fellowship requires preparation for that fellowship. He cannot eat with you if you do not have anything prepared. It takes time away from other things to have fellowship.

[1 Corinthians 10:16: The cup of blessing that we bless, is it not a sharing [communion] in the blood of Christ? The bread that we break, is it not a sharing [communion] in the body of Christ?]

The word "sharing" is the same Greek word as fellowship in 1 John 1. The Greek word is "*koinOnia*". It means "common". Not common as in "a frequent occurrence" or "mediocre", but as having something "in common". This is talking about a close association involving mutual interest or sharing. It is from the same word that we get "Koine" Greek, which is "common Greek". It is talking about communion with one another. This type of communion is a meditating on things in the past as well as hopes for the future that are shared in common. When we participate in the breaking of bread and drinking of the cup, it is a time of remembering His death in the past and reflecting on the hope of glory in His coming Kingdom; it is communion.

[2 Corinthians 6:14: Do not be mismatched [unequally yoked] with unbelievers. For what partnership is there between righteousness and lawlessness? Or what fellowship [koinOnia] is there between light and darkness?]

Being "unequally yoked together" is to be mismatched. This expression "unequally yoked" is only found here in the NT. It is not found in classical Greek, it is not in the LXX, but a similar adjective that means "of a diverse kind" is found in Leviticus 19:19.

"Unequally" or "mismatched" doesn't give the full flavor of this word. It is not simply an inequality, but a complete difference in kind. This figure of speech comes from the prohibition in Deuteronomy 22:10 against yoking together two different animals. The reference in this verse is generic and covers all forms of intimacy and is not limited to marriage. It applies to business partners, close friends, and even family in some cases.

When talking about fellowship, there are five different words that describe different shades of fellowship.

[2 Corinthians 6:14: Do not be mismatched with unbelievers. For what partnership is there between righteousness and lawlessness? Or what fellowship [koinOnia] is there between light and darkness?]

The word "partnership" carries the thought of participation. If you are in the light, you can have fellowship with those who are in the light. If you are in darkness, you can have fellowship with those who are in darkness. If you are in the light can you have fellowship with those who are in darkness? No!

[1 John 1:6-7: If we say that we have fellowship [koinOnia] with him while we are walking in darkness, we lie and do not do what is true; but if we walk in the light as he himself is in the light, we have fellowship [koinOnia] with one another, and the blood of Jesus his Son cleanses us from all sin.]

[Galatians 2:9: and when James and Cephas and John, who were acknowledged pillars, recognized the grace that had been given to me, they gave to Barnabas and me the right hand of fellowship, agreeing that we should go to the Gentiles and they to the circumcised.]

Fellowship begins with reaching out to each other, and this happened in this passage when the "pillars of the church" recognized the grace that had been given to Paul and Barnabas. You have to reach out if you want fellowship.

Have you ever reached out to shake someone's hand and they refused to reach out to you? This type of behavior destroys the opportunity for fellowship. Sometimes this can be for a good reason if someone wants to show they are denying the hand of fellowship.[16] Giving the right hand of fellowship is reaching out to touch and be close. The grace that had been given was recognized on the basis of doctrine.

[2 Peter 1:2: May grace and peace be yours in abundance in the knowledge [epignosis] of God and of Jesus our Lord.]

Knowledge comes from doctrine.

---

[16] There was a good example of this a few years back when Bill Clinton gave a Medal of Honor to a soldier posthumously. The father accepted the medal for his son, but refused to shake Bill Clinton's Hand, as it was Bill Clinton's actions in emasculating our military that led to his son's death.

[Malachi 3:16-18: Then those who revered the LORD spoke with one another. The LORD took note and listened, and a book of remembrance was written before him of those who revered the LORD and thought on his name. They shall be mine, says the LORD of hosts, my special possession on the day when I act, and I will spare them as parents spare their children who serve them. Then once more you shall see the difference between the righteous and the wicked, between one who serves God and one who does not serve him.]

Fellowship with other believers promotes thinking about the Lord and the Lord wants to remember that fellowship. He writes it down in his book of remembrance. What promotes the fear of the Lord? Doctrine. Doctrine promotes the fear of the Lord, and the fear of the Lord encourages us to think upon the Lord's name.

Fellowship demonstrates acceptance, and that encourages anyone. Paul and Barnabas felt this fellowship and acceptance, even though there were those who had doctrinal differences with them.

You can have fellowship with someone even if you do not agree with him in every area. If you have the desire to come to an understanding of the Truth, you may never come to an agreement on some things. Not because you do not care but because you have a different understanding. When you no longer care, there is no room for fellowship

However, there has to be that common bond of coming to an understanding of Truth. A faithful believer cannot have fellowship with one who is lawless.

The word "*koinOnia*" is translated as "common" in some translations, which is what is implied with the word.

[Jude 1:3: Beloved, while eagerly preparing to write to you about the salvation **_we share_** [*koinOnia*], I find it necessary to write and appeal to you to contend for the faith that was once for all entrusted to the saints']

[KJV Jude 1:3a: Beloved, when I gave all diligence to write unto you of the common [*koinOnia*] salvation...]

[CLV Jude 1:3: Beloved, giving all diligence to be writing to you concerning our common [*koinOnia*] salvation and life...]

If you are in the family of God, this is something we all have in common. This salvation is the salvation that everyone in the body of Christ has fellowship in. This salvation is the birth from above in John 3:3.

[Titus 1:4: To Titus, my loyal child in the faith we share [*koinOnia*]: Grace and peace from God the Father and Christ Jesus our Savior.]

This passage introduces us to fellowship in faith. This goes beyond our common salvation and has to do with pleasing God.

[Hebrews 11:6: And without faith it is impossible to please God, for whoever would approach him must believe that he exists and that he **_rewards_** those who **_seek_** [present tense; are seeking] him.]

This is not our common salvation, this is rewards for faithfulness. Our rewards are our inheritance.

[Colossians 3:24: since you know that from the Lord you will receive the inheritance as your reward; you serve the Lord Christ. For the wrongdoer will be paid back for whatever wrong has been done, and there is no partiality.]

Paul and Titus were pleasing God, so they had fellowship in that lifestyle. Fellowship of faith can only be enjoyed by those who have not departed from the faith, or made shipwreck of the faith.

Making shipwreck of the faith or departing from the faith does not mean a loss of being in the family. After all, a child cannot be unborn. But departing from the faith or making shipwreck of the faith has to do with rewards or inheritance.

[Acts 2:44: All who believed [present tense; all who are believing] were together and had all things in common [*koinos*].]

All these are believing and they are together. "Believe" in the present tense is synonymous with "faith". These are living a lifestyle that is pleasing to God and they were sharing with those who were in need. This is two points of fellowship. Having fellowship together helps us to share in each other's needs. They were not being frivolous with their stuff, but they were willing to give up their stuff to help others with whom they were having fellowship.

[Romans 15:26: for Macedonia and Achaia have been pleased to share their resources [make contribution; *koinOnia*] with the poor among the saints at Jerusalem.]

We can have fellowship through giving.

[2 Corinthians 8:3-4: For, as I can testify, they voluntarily gave according to their means, and even beyond their means, begging us earnestly for the privilege [grace] of sharing [fellowship; *koinOnia*] in this ministry to the saints...]

We can have fellowship with missionaries by ministering to them financially.

[Philippians 1:5: [I thank my God] because of your sharing [contribution; fellowship; *koinonia*] in the gospel from the first day until now.]

This example of fellowship is a church that ministered to Paul financially.

[2 Corinthians 8:23-24: As for Titus, he is my partner [*koinOninos*] and co-worker in your service; as for our brothers, they are messengers [apostles] of the churches, the glory of Christ. Therefore openly before the churches, show them the proof of your love and of our reason for boasting about you.]

[Philemon 1:17: [Talking about Onesimus] So if you consider me your partner [*koinOnia*], welcome him as you would welcome me.]

There is fellowship among those who are working and co-laboring in the ministry.

[Philippians 3:10: I want to know Christ and the power of his resurrection and the sharing [fellowship; *koinonia*] of his sufferings by becoming like him in his death...]

We have fellowship in suffering. The Bible is clear on one thing: If you live a godly life, you _**will**_ suffer in this life.

[Philippians 1:29: For he has graciously granted you the privilege not only of believing [present, active; being faithful] in Christ, but of suffering for him as well.]

It is not easy to suffer, but sometimes we need to. If a brother is suffering, we need to enter into his suffering, even if it causes us to suffer also. The way we enter into Christ's suffering is to participate in the suffering of others.

If we are alone and we are not in fellowship with other brothers and sisters, we can become discouraged and quit. We have a coach who is exhorting us!

[Ecclesiastes 4:9-10: Two are better than one, because they have a good reward for their toil. For if they fall, one will lift up the other; but woe to one who is alone and falls and does not have another to help.]

Solomon really knew what he was talking about! Fellowship is important because _**we need the encouragement of others!**_

Fellowship helps us in our walk of obedience because we have the encouragement of others. The foundation of this communion is our common salvation. When rightly divided, the issue of whether salvation is permanent or not is easily understood.

Why then is there so much confusion over this issue? Because of the failure of our preachers and teachers to teach that man is a trichotomous being and not a dichotomous one. Teaching that man is a dichotomous being is the teaching of natural evolution and not the teaching of God. The theory of natural evolution holds that man, being merely an animal, is only a body and a soul *or* spirit: a life-force.

[1 Thessalonians 5:23: May [optative; probable failure] the God of peace himself sanctify you entirely; and may [optative] your spirit *and* soul *and* body be kept sound [complete] and blameless at the coming of our Lord Jesus Christ.]

In 1 Thessalonians 5:23, the Bible teaches us that man is a spirit *and* a soul *and* a body.

[Hebrews 4:12: Indeed, the word of God is living and active, sharper than any two-edged sword, piercing until it divides *soul from spirit*, joints from marrow; it is able to judge the thoughts and intentions[17] of the heart.]

In both of these verses "soul" is *psuche* and "spirit" is *pneuma*; they are distinct and different. Scripture teaches that Jesus was born in the image of His creation, and when he died on the cross His spirit went up into heaven, his soul went to *Sheol*, and his body went into the tomb of Joseph of Arimethea.[18]

The book of Hebrews is dealing primarily with the present aspect of salvation and the future salvation which is the result of the present. The past aspect is not ignored, but just as in the rest of the Bible, the present and future aspects of salvation are given positions of much more importance. The past tense of salvation is rarely spoken of throughout the NT, but the present tense is greatly emphasized.

---

[17] As a reminder, although God judges intentions, it is direction, not intention, which determine the destination.

[18] See Luke 23:46, Acts 2:27, and Mark 15:46, among other passages.

The past tense of salvation is being born from above into the family of God. The present tense of salvation is related to rewards for faithfulness; it is about wages and it involves works. We do not work to obtain our common salvation, maintain our common salvation, or to prove we are saved, but we work in order to be faithful and we have been promised great things for being faithful.[19]

The five warning passages of Hebrews are written to believers. There is nothing in the book of Hebrews, or anywhere else in the Bible that even hints that we can lose our common salvation. We cannot be unborn from above.

They do, however, serve as warnings against the very real possibility that we can lose our rewards or our inheritance in the coming Kingdom. These rewards are also called "salvation" [20] and have been offered to those who are faithful and obedient, and if we are unfaithful and disobedient, we will still be rewarded, but we will not like those rewards.

The warnings in the book of Hebrews serve to admonish us to press on and obtain the inheritance that God has promised to those who are faithful. The faithful are the overcomers or prevailers. These things will be revealed at the Judgment Seat of Christ, and they represent the very real possibility that there will be negative consequences for those who are not faithful.

---

[19] It is also important to keep in mind that there is a major difference between being saved from something and being saved out of something. If you are saved *from* (*apo*) a pit, you are kept from falling into it. If you are saved *out of* (*ek*) a pit, you have to be in the pit in the first place.
[20] This is obviously not the same salvation covered in Acts 16:31.

The book of Hebrews is very controversial. Or perhaps it would be better to say that man has created so much controversy surrounding the book of Hebrews that it has become controversial. There are many who call this book the "riddle of the NT".

It seems probable that Paul wrote this book, but that cannot be proved. In the other epistles he "signed" them with an introduction which identified him. This one was not "signed". There are those who believe that Luke, James, Apollos or Barnabas wrote this book. In Hebrews 13:23, the writer calls Timothy "brother", therefore the writer was closely acquainted with Timothy. Whoever wrote this book had a great understanding of the work of Christ and was well versed in the OT.[21]

The writer is writing to Jews and encouraging and admonishing them in their persecution. Because of the controversy surrounding Paul and the attitude many Jews had about him, it is very likely that if he wrote this epistle, he would have kept it anonymous in order that those reading or hearing the message would not shut their ears to the message.

The admonitions and encouragements are not in question; these are very real warnings. What is in question is the nature of the warnings in this book. Are they written to people who are really saved and in the family of God? Are they written for casual bystanders who might be listening in? What is the real threat for failing to prevail? Can you become unsaved?

---

[21] Pun intended.

At the beginning of this study we looked at the five warning passages in this book: Hebrews 2:1-5, 3:7-4:13, 6:4-8, 10:26-39, and 12:25-29.

[Hebrews 13:22: I appeal to you, brothers and sisters, bear with my word of exhortation, for I have written to you briefly.]

This verse tells us that this epistle is written to the brothers and sisters, and the brothers and sisters are those who are doing the will of the Father. These warnings are not written to all people, but are written to all who read the epistle; the warnings are to those who are being faithful. These warnings are written to those who would be prevailers and conquerors, and not merely survivors.

Although this seems to be stated quite clearly, it is still a very controversial belief. People will argue about whether these warnings apply to believers or non-believers. They will argue whether the writer assumed some of his readers would be unbelievers, or whether they were all believers, or whether they were "professors and not possessors", or any of a number of other man-made controversies.

The third warning in Hebrews 6:4-8 is one of the most heavily debated passages in the entire Bible! There are at least a dozen distinct views on this passage, of which I am aware, and probably many more. Almost all of these arguments present themselves as "our side vs their side". Before you say, "oh, no, a dozen!" we are not going to look at all of these arguments. We are only interested in three of the basic ones, of which the rest are derivations. The three basic views are: The Arminian view, the Calvinist view, and the Truth. (We will call this latter, the Partaker view from chapter 3, or the Partner view. The word "partaker" or "partner" is from the Greek word *metochoi*, and indicates an even closer relationship than "brother".)

The Calvinist view basically says that these warnings are addressed to "professors, not possessors". They are not really saved. They did not **_really_** believe. They are phony believers, so are not really believers at all. They did not really believe. There are many different flavors of Calvinism, but this is a fairly simple and accurate look at the Calvinist approach.

This view comes from Calvinism which is built around five points (TULIP[22]) and the points build upon each other until it gets to the last point which is "perseverance of the saints". This means that all "true believers" will never deny their faith, nor will they behave in a manner that is contrary to what God commands, although most of them are pretty fuzzy on exactly where the line of too much sin is. This concept of not really believing is called "experimental predestinarianism", or temporary faith. In other words, God gives them a taste of His grace, but he never really intends to give them the grace to follow through with "real" faith.

What those who hold this view believe is, if one is **_really_** saved, he will persevere. If one is **_really_** saved, his works will prove it. That is the test. They say that without good works, you are not really saved. Calvinism denies the assurance of the common salvation, which is in essence calling the Bible faulty. The proof of their salvation (whether they really, **_really_**, **_REALLY_** believed or not) is always in the future. They say that no one can ever really know if he truly believed enough to possess eternal life or not. There are many modern preachers pushing this view under the form of neo-Puritanism.

---

[22] Total depravity, Unconditional Election, Limited atonement, Irresistible grace, Preservation of the Saints.

I have one thing to say to that: Works are works are works; it does not matter if you say you have to work to get saved, to stay saved, or to prove you are saved, they are still works!

The Arminian view readily admits that these warnings are written to those who are really saved currently, but these believers are in grave danger of becoming unborn! The work of Jesus on the cross just was not quite enough. To the Arminian, the common salvation (being born from above) can be undone. They do not put their faith in Christ alone and his work on the cross. To the Arminian point of view, the believer's security rests in Christ's work *plus* the individual's decision to remain faithful and not fall away. They admit that one is not born into the family through works, but works are central to making sure you remain in the family. Acts 16:31 does not say, "Believe on the Lord Jesus and continue in good works without falling away and you just might be saved if you do enough of those good works to prove it", it says "believe and you *will be* saved"!

Both the Calvinist and Arminian views recognize the core truth that the work of Christ is necessary. Both recognize the importance of works in the lives of believers. Both erroneously place a great importance on works for the believer to continue in common salvation in order to get into heaven.

Yet with all these similarities, these two sides have been duking it out with each other for centuries! They seem to be on opposite sides but are not really that far apart and both are teaching the grave error of salvation through works.

The view in which we are most interested is the Truth: The Partaker or Partner view. This view is in agreement with the

Calvinist view that the life one receives through being born from above cannot be forfeited because that is what the Bible says. This view is also in agreement with the Arminian view that says the subjects of the warnings in Hebrews are truly believers.

Does this create a contradictory viewpoint? Not at all!

The Truth tells us that these warnings are written to believers who are in danger of losing their rewards, but they cannot lose their familial status. They are in the family and cannot be removed, but they can lose their position *within* the family and be moved to a lower position.

The Truth tells us that works are not proof of being born from above, neither are they the means by which that common salvation is secured or kept.[23] The Truth tells us that we obtain the common salvation by believing in the Lord Jesus. *Plus nothing!*

Works are not in view at all in relation to being born from above. Security (remaining in the family) is a reality and is assured to those who believe. It is based solely upon the finished work of the Christ upon the cross. It is free to us.

This view of the Truth as it relates to these warning passages lets the text speak without making up or adding anything, and does not require ignoring the content and the context.

One key to understanding these warnings is to understand that they are separate, but they all go together as a single whole. These are five separate warnings, but they are united. All five must be

---

[23] Oh, isn't it terrible? He was one good work short of being really and truly saved!

put together like a chain puzzle. They complement one another as they increase in severity. Each warning builds upon the previous, and each increases in intensity until the last warning, which serves as the culmination of all the warnings, to declare the ultimate and drastic consequences for those who do not prevail.

As with everything in the Bible, this is all built upon the foundation of everything else in the Bible. It is the holographic image we have discussed in the past. The writer uses the types that we are given in the Exodus generation. The Children of Israel were a redeemed people that were disobedient to God – they did not prevail – and they were judged for that behavior.

The story of the Exodus is used as a type in each of these five warnings. I would encourage each of you to reread the story of the Exodus and familiarize yourself with the story for the sake of this study in Hebrews. The story of the Exodus emphasizes the danger of unbelief toward God and failing to prevail. If we keep in mind the unity of the types of the Exodus generation we will see the unity of the antitypes in the warnings in Hebrews, and many of the difficulties in understanding this book will disappear.

Text without context is a pretext. If we are to properly interpret any passage in the Bible, we must determine the context. In the epistles, the beginning of each one determines the context. Hebrews chapter 1 provides the introduction, as well as the outline for all five warning passages. As we have seen, the foundation is the key to understanding that which has been built upon in it, from Genesis 1:1 all the way through Revelation 22:21. The same is true here: The key to the book of Hebrews is given to us in chapter 1.

[Hebrews 1:1a: Long ago God spoke…]

That pretty much sums up the revelation that God has given to man. God spoke the universe into existence. Both his Word and his words are powerful.

[Genesis 1:1-3,6,9,11,14-15,20,24,26: In the beginning when God created the heavens and the earth, the earth was a formless void and darkness covered the face of the deep, while a wind from God swept over the face of the waters. Then God said, "Let there be light"; and there was light… And God said, "Let there be a dome in the midst of the waters, and let it separate the waters from the waters"… And God said, "Let the waters under the sky be gathered together into one place, and let the dry land appear"… And God said, "Let there be lights in the dome of the sky to separate the day from the night; and let them be for signs[24] and for seasons and for days and years, and let them be lights in the dome of the sky to give light upon the earth"… And God said, "Let the waters bring forth swarms of living creatures, and let birds fly above the earth across the dome of the sky"… And God said, "Let the earth bring forth living creatures of every kind: cattle and creeping things and wild animals of the earth of every kind"… Then God said, "Let us make humankind in our image, according to our likeness."]

God spoke, and it was so, and it was so, and it was so, and it was so, and it was so, and it was so.

John 1:1 tells us that Jesus is the Word made manifest.

---

[24] And this message keeps speaking to us today!

[John 1:1-5: In the beginning was the Word, and the Word was with God, and the Word was God. He was in the beginning with God. All things came into being through him, and without him not one thing came into being. What has come into being in him was life, and the life was the light of all people. The light shines in the darkness, and the darkness did not overcome it.]

[Hebrews 1:1-4: Long ago God spoke to our ancestors in many and various ways by the prophets, but in these last days he has spoken to us by a Son [*the* Son], whom he appointed heir of all things, through whom he also created the worlds. He is the reflection of God's glory and the exact imprint of God's very being, and he sustains all things by his powerful word [spoken word, not *logos*][25]. When he had made purification for sins, he sat down at the right hand of the Majesty on high, having become as much superior to angels as the name he has inherited is more excellent than theirs.]

God spoke. The Son is also deity. Everything was created through the Son, and the Son reflects the glory of God. The Son is the image of the Father on the Earth. The Son is the *Logos* and now he is seated at the right hand of the Father awaiting ***that*** day which is coming.

[Hebrews 1:5-14: For to which of the angels did God ever say, "You are my Son; today I have begotten you"? Or again, "I will

---

[25] In John 1:1 and 14, Revelation 19:13, and 1 John 1:1, the term "*Logos*" is applied to the Christ. This comes from "*lego*", which means to lay by or to collect. In other words to put words side by side in order to express an entire statement. "*Logos*" is used for reason as well as speech. The Stoics used it in reference to the soul of the world and Marcus Aurelius used "*spermatikos logos*" as the generative principle in nature. Heraclitus used it for the idea that controls the universe. "*Logos*" implies the complete idea that is stated and not simply the words that are spoken.

be his Father, and he will be my Son"? And again, when he brings the firstborn into the world, he says, "Let all God's angels worship him." Of the angels he says, "He makes his angels winds, and his servants flames of fire." But of the Son he says, "Your throne, O God, is forever and ever, and the righteous scepter is the scepter of your kingdom. You have loved righteousness and hated wickedness; therefore God, your God, has anointed you with the oil of gladness beyond your companions." And, "In the beginning, Lord, you founded the earth, and the heavens are the work of your hands; they will perish, but you remain; they will all wear out like clothing; like a cloak you will roll them up, and like clothing they will be changed. But you are the same, and your years will never end." But to which of the angels has he ever said, "Sit at my right hand until I make your enemies a footstool for your feet"? Are not all angels spirits in the divine service, sent to serve for the sake of those who are to inherit salvation?]

This passage contains seven quotations from the OT that are Messianic in nature. The writer did not use these passages as proof texts, he used them as background texts. You are expected to understand the background. These passages point to the coming Kingdom:

1. "You are my Son; today I have begotten you…" (Quoted from Psalm 2:7.)
2. "I will be his Father, and he will be my Son…" (Quoted from 2 Samuel 7:14.)
3. When he brings the firstborn into the world, he says, "Let all God's angels worship him." (Quoted from the LXX version of Deuteronomy 32:43. It is not found in the Hebrew.)

4. Of the angels he says, "He makes his angels winds, and his servants flames of fire." (Quoted from Psalm 104:4.)
5. But of the Son he says, "Your throne, O God, is forever and ever, and the righteous scepter is the scepter of your kingdom. You have loved righteousness and hated wickedness; therefore God, your God, has anointed you with the oil of gladness beyond your companions." (Quoted from Psalm 45:7.)
6. "In the beginning, Lord, you founded the earth, and the heavens are the work of your hands; they will perish, but you remain; they will all wear out like clothing; like a cloak you will roll them up, and like clothing they will be changed. But you are the same, and your years will never end." (Quoted from the LXX version of Psalm 102:26-28. It is not found in the Hebrew.)
7. But to which of the angels has he ever said, "Sit at my right hand until I make your enemies a footstool for your feet"? (Quoted from Psalm 110:1.)

In chapter 1, there is great importance placed upon the idea of heirship and inheritance. Inheritance is mentioned three different times in the 14 verses we just read.

In verse 2, the son is appointed heir of all things. In verse 4, he has become "as much superior to angels as the name he has inherited is more excellent than theirs". In verse 14, angels are ministers to those who shall inherit salvation.

We are shown how Jesus the Christ is superior, and how he has revealed the things of God far better than the patriarchs and prophets ever could.

Verse 14 is of great importance to us in this study.

56

[Hebrews 1:14: Are not all angels spirits in the divine service, sent to serve for the sake of those who are to inherit salvation?]

Here we see a group of people who are about to inherit salvation. Who are these people? What is the nature of this salvation?

The future is in view. They shall inherit, they are going to inherit, they are to inherit; this is future. This is not talking about the common salvation which we can possess in the present, which is based upon a past event.

Verse 9 speaks of his companions. His companions are those who will participate in the coming Kingdom; the partners or partakers. By implication, it is referring to those who are reading this passage.

This is why it is vital to understand the multiple facets of salvation, and apply them properly to interpreting the Bible. The future aspect has to do with our inheritance or rewards. It has to do with the coming Kingdom. Only those who already possess the present tense salvation (the common salvation) can receive the salvation being spoken of here. Only those who are already in the family can possibly be in a position to inherit.

The present tense salvation requires nothing but "believe on the Lord Jesus". This future salvation spoken of in Hebrews requires faith and works. "Those who are about to inherit" are believers who are already in the family.

This first chapter sets the tone and scope of the entire book of Hebrews and the entire book focuses on prophetic and spiritual truths concerning the coming Messianic rule of the Lord. This first chapter contains seven quotations from the Old Testament that prophesy about the Lord and his coming glory.

Seven is the number that refers to completion. Paul used seven Messianic quotes in chapter 1. Throughout the book of Hebrews, he gives seven titles to refer to the Christ in order to give the complete image of Jesus as Messiah:

1. Heir of all things (1:2)
2. Pioneer or Captain of our salvation (2:10)
3. Apostle and High Priest (3:1)
4. The Source or Author of salvation (5:9)
5. Forerunner (6:20)
6. High Priest (10:21)
7. The Author and Finisher of our faith (12:2)

This picture that is being presented shows the way for what is covered in the rest of the book. These titles and Messianic quotes are not given as proof that Jesus is the Messiah, they simply emphasize the coming Kingdom and show who Jesus is.

Paul devotes a lot of attention to the coming Kingdom and it is not something which we should take lightly.

[1 Corinthians 15:20-28: But in fact Christ has been raised from the dead,[26] the first fruits of those who have died. For since death came through a human being, the resurrection of the dead has also come through a human being; for as all die in Adam, so all will be made alive in Christ. But each in his own order: Christ the first fruits, then at his coming those who belong to Christ. Then comes the end [rest], when he hands over the kingdom to

---

[26] Out from among the dead. The out-resurrection. This idea is a lengthy study on its own.

God the Father, after he has destroyed every ruler and every authority and power. For he must reign until he has put all his enemies under his feet. The last enemy to be destroyed is death. For "God has put all things in subjection under his feet." But when it says, "All things are put in subjection," it is plain that this does not include the one who put all things in subjection under him. When all things are subjected to him, then the Son himself will also be subjected to the one who put all things in subjection under him, so that God may be all in all.]

He "must reign" in order to defeat all enemies. His redemptive work is not finished! This work will continue into the coming Kingdom!

All of prophecy points to this coming Kingdom. Entrance, or enjoying the full allotment in the coming Kingdom centers on our behavior; it has to do with our faithfulness. These five warnings in the book of Hebrews stand there like big flashing neon signs warning us of dangers that will prevent us from receiving our full allotment potential.

Why are warnings used? Why not just tell us of the glory of Christ and how perfect it will be in heaven? Why not just tell us of his superiority to angels and how much he loves us all and let it go at that?

Because if we do not prevail, we are in serious danger!

The Alaska Railroad has beautiful trains with very nice amenities, but there are warnings around the tracks and the crossings. You can be in danger if you do not follow the rules.

Simply put, if there were no danger, there would be no need of warnings.

Since God saw fit to give us warnings, we know that God loves us enough to tell us the rules of the game. In his mercy, God had the writer of this book warn the readers about these very real dangers. Ultimately, these warnings reach beyond the original readers and hits us right in the heart.

To reiterate: These warnings are written to believers who are already in the family. We must not pick and choose which passages in Hebrews applies to those who are really and truly saved and which ones applies to those who are professors and not possessors. Those arguments are fallacies. Of course, there are those who always try to find some way to apply _**all**_ warnings to someone other than themselves. In the book of Hebrews, the writer includes himself in the warnings several times. Apostasy is a very real danger, and there are dire consequences for apostasy. "Apostasy" means to fall away. You cannot fall away from a plane, unless you are on the plane.

Hebrews is not about "getting people saved". It is not about blessings of children or adding more children to the family. It is about bringing sons (mature; sons and daughters) to glory. It is about inheritance and rewards. And like Reuben or Esau, we stand a very real danger of losing our potential inheritance.

The First Warning: Hebrews 2:1-5

[Hebrews 2:1-5: Therefore we must pay greater attention to what we have heard, so that we do not drift away from it. For if the message declared through angels was valid, and every transgression or disobedience received a just penalty, how can we escape if we neglect so great a salvation? It was declared at first through the Lord, and it was attested to us by those who heard him, while God added his testimony by signs and wonders and various miracles, and by gifts of the Holy Spirit, distributed according to his will. Now God did not subject the coming world, about which we are speaking, to angels.]

This passage begins with, "Therefore we". Any time you see a "therefore", it is "there for" a reason. In this passage, it points us back to what was said in chapter one, which is the foundation for the entire epistle. It points to the coming Millennial glory of the Christ, and the coming inheritance and glory of the faithful believer in the coming Kingdom. It is telling us, "Keep what we just studied in your mind".

Notice that it says "we". The writer includes himself in this exhortation. "How can we escape, if we neglect so great a salvation?"

What are the results of neglecting the "so great salvation" and what is the "so great salvation"?

The great salvation refers back to the salvation in chapter 1:14. It has to do with our inheritance. "So great" is from a word that means "great, important, and mighty", but only in reference _to degree_. It is compared to something else, not compared to a general value. Compared to a $1 bill, a $100 bill is "so great", but you would not refuse a $1 bill if I offered it to you, would you?

The "so great" salvation has to do with ruling and reigning with Christ. It has to do with inheriting or entering the Kingdom. Those who are found worthy at the Judgment Seat will be those who will be in positions of authority. This is the hope of glory.

This is what the writer has in view in verse 5, which he calls the "coming world" [the age to come]. This is a time in which the angels, who presently rule, will be replaced by Jesus the Christ and his comrades. His comrades are those who are being faithful in this age and are about to inherit salvation in the coming age.

[Ephesians 6:12: For our struggle is not against enemies of blood and flesh, but against the rulers, against the authorities, against the cosmic powers of this present darkness, against the spiritual forces of evil in the heavenly places.]

[Revelation 12:7-9: And war broke out in heaven; Michael and his angels fought against the dragon. The dragon and his angels fought back, but they were defeated, and there was no longer any place for them in heaven. The great dragon was thrown down, that ancient serpent, who is called the Devil and Satan, the deceiver of the whole world—he was thrown down to the earth, and his angels were thrown down with him.]

If you neglect this salvation, there will be serious consequences. "We shall not escape." What shall we not escape? We shall not escape the just recompense of reward, which is spoken of in verse 2. Note that this salvation is a reward, just as its loss is a reward, so this is not referring to a loss of our common salvation, which is given freely based upon nothing but "believe".

[Hebrews 2:2: For if the message declared through angels was valid, and every transgression or disobedience received a just penalty...][27]

---

[27] In the NRSV the word "penalty" does not fully convey the meaning of the word. It is translated from a long word that is a real mouthful – *misthapodosian* – which comes from two words, "wages" and "pay off". The same word is

When the Lord assumes the role of Judge, what is the first group that he will judge? Believers!

[1 Peter 4:17-19: For the time has come for judgment to begin with the household of God; if it begins with us, what will be the end for those who do not obey the gospel of God? And "If it is hard for the righteous to be saved, what will become of the ungodly and the sinners?"]

At the Judgment Seat of Christ, he will be rewarding believers according to their works. It is only believers in view here, and "rewards" are not simply goodies handed out. Rewards are not always pleasant rewards. These rewards are what you have earned.

[Colossians 3:23-25: Whatever your task, put yourselves into it, as done for the Lord and not for your masters, since you know that from the Lord you will receive the inheritance as your reward; you serve the Lord Christ. For the wrongdoer will be paid back for whatever wrong has been done, and there is no partiality.]

The reward is an inheritance.[28] That means it is a family matter.

Those who do well will receive for the good they have done. Those who do wrong will receive for the wrong they have done. Some erroneously think this reward will simply be missing out on good stuff, but the reality is the danger is much more severe.

---

used whether for good or bad, but it is what you have earned. In this case, it is a "just penalty", but it is much deeper than that.

[28] Remember, there is a birth inheritance which we cannot lose and a reward inheritance which we can lose.

This can go so far as chastisement and not merely losing out on what could have been obtained. We know we cannot lose our common salvation, but we do stand to lose much or even be punished.

This first warning in Hebrews is warning us to beware this negative "reward"!

The Second Warning: Hebrews 3:7-4:13

[Hebrews 3:7-4:13: Therefore, as the Holy Spirit says, "Today, if you hear his voice, do not harden your hearts as in the rebellion, as on the day of testing in the wilderness, where your ancestors put me to the test, though they had seen my works for forty years. Therefore I was angry with that generation, and I said, 'They always go astray in their hearts, and they have not known my ways.' As in my anger I swore, 'They will not enter my rest.' " Take care, brothers and sisters, that none of you may have an evil, unbelieving heart that turns away from the living God. But exhort one another every day, as long as it is called "today," so that none of you may be hardened by the deceitfulness of sin. For we have become partners of Christ, if only we hold our first confidence firm to the end. As it is said, "Today, if you hear his voice, do not harden your hearts as in the rebellion."

Now who were they who heard and yet were rebellious? Was it not all those who left Egypt under the leadership of Moses? But with whom was he angry forty years? Was it not those who sinned, whose bodies fell in the wilderness? And to whom did he swear that they would not enter his rest, if not to those who were disobedient? So we see that they were unable to enter because of unbelief.

Therefore, while the promise of entering his rest is still open, let us take care that none of you should seem to have failed to reach it. For indeed the good news came to us just as to them; but the message they heard did not benefit them, because they were not united by faith with those who listened. For we who have believed enter that rest, just as God has said, "As in my anger I swore, 'They shall not enter my rest,' " though his works were finished at the foundation of the world. For in one place it speaks about the seventh day as follows, "And God rested on the seventh day from all his works." And again in this place it says, "They shall not enter my rest." Since therefore it remains open for some to enter it, and those who formerly received the good news failed to enter because of disobedience, again he sets a certain day— "today"—saying through David much later, in the words already quoted, "Today, if you hear his voice, do not harden your hearts."

For if Joshua had given them rest, God would not speak later about another day. So then, a sabbath rest still remains for the people of God; for those who enter God's rest also cease from their labors as God did from his. Let us therefore make every effort to enter that rest, so that no one may fall through such disobedience as theirs.

Indeed, the word of God is living and active, sharper than any two-edged sword, piercing until it divides soul from spirit, joints from marrow; it is able to judge the thoughts and intentions of the heart. And before him no creature is hidden, but all are naked and laid bare to the eyes of the one to whom we must render an account.]

Between Hebrews 2:5 and 3:7, the writer of this epistle once again discusses the glory of Jesus, and what he did for his brothers and sisters, and how God made him the pioneer of their salvation through his sufferings.[29]

[Hebrews 2:11-15: For the one who sanctifies and those who are sanctified all have one Father. For this reason Jesus is not ashamed to call them brothers and sisters, saying, "I will proclaim your name to my brothers and sisters, in the midst of the congregation I will praise you.

And again, "I will put my trust in him."

And again, "Here am I and the children whom God has given me."

Since, therefore, the children share flesh and blood, he himself likewise shared the same things, so that through death he might destroy the one who has the power of death, that is, the devil, and free those who all their lives were held in slavery by the fear of death. For it is clear that he did not come to help angels, but the descendants of Abraham.]

The first Adam lost the right to rule the Earth; the second Adam regained that right for us. We now have that future potential, through Jesus the Christ.

Many ask, "But are we not in that Kingdom now?"

No!

---

[29] Some translations call him the "author" of salvation, but that misses the fact that he precedes the brethren. The word has the idea of leader or captain or pioneer.

Many declare we are in that Kingdom now, while it may be in the near future, that Kingdom is yet future.

We may have allied ourselves with Jesus and placed ourselves in that position, just as those around David allied themselves with him while Saul still ruled, but Jesus has not yet taken charge. He came as prophet, he is now our high priest, but his office as king has yet to be fulfilled!

Satan is the god of this age. He has dominion of the spiritual realm of the Earth. He is the prince and the power of the air.

[2 Corinthians 4:3-4: And even if our gospel is veiled, it is veiled to those who are perishing. In their case the god of this world has blinded the minds of the unbelievers, to keep them from seeing the light of the gospel of the glory of Christ, who is the image of God.]

[Ephesians 2:1-2: You were dead through the trespasses and sins in which you once lived, following the course of this world, following the ruler of the power of the air, the spirit that is now at work among those who are disobedient.]

[John 12:27-31: Now my soul is troubled. And what should I say—'Father, save me from this hour'? No, it is for this reason that I have come to this hour. Father, glorify your name." Then a voice came from heaven, "I have glorified it, and I will glorify it again." The crowd standing there heard it and said that it was thunder. Others said, "An angel has spoken to him." Jesus answered, "This voice has come for your sake, not for mine. Now is [present tense] the judgment of this world; now the ruler of this world will [future, passive] be driven out.]

This entire passage focuses upon one thing: The purpose for which man was created, which is to rule and reign. In order to rule and reign, you must be *fit* to rule and reign.

This warning, like the first warning, focuses upon the potential loss of inheritance. At the risk of sounding like a broken record, *inheritance is a family matter*.[30]

In ancient Israel, the firstborn was to be the "ruler" of the family. However, just as Reuben lost the right of the firstborn, we can also lose that right, and someone else can take our place. Reuben was still in the family, but he forfeited the better inheritance.

This passage in Hebrews uses the example of the Children of Israel in the Exodus generation. They had been brought out to rule and reign, but they blew it! They were a redeemed people, they were delivered out of Egypt by the power of God whose power was made manifest to them: The firstborn were saved by the blood of the Passover lamb,[31] they were baptized in the Red Sea, God destroyed their enemies that were pursuing them, they were fed manna daily, and when they complained about that, God gave them quail.

After all this, the spies went into the land that was promised to them and came back and said, "We can't do it". Everyone decided it was time to go back to Egypt.

---

[30] Take a big, red pen and write "inheritance is a family matter" in the front of your Bible and write it every time you find a passage about inheritance.

[31] *All* the Jews were in the family; the Passover lamb was for everyone to partake, but the blood was shed only for the firstborn. This is about position within the family.

All but Joshua and Caleb; Joshua and Caleb had faith and they were faithful.

The rest lost their inheritance. They were still in the family (they were saved), but they did not have all they could have. They were in the land of Promise, but they did not enter in to the better part of that inheritance.

Genesis 15:18 tells us that the land of promise was from the Nile to the Euphrates, and was conditioned upon nothing but being in the family. They were in that land of promise before they even left Goshen. However, the better part of their inheritance, the Land Flowing with Milk and Honey, was conditioned upon faithfulness.

The Children of Israel saw firsthand the power of God: They were surrounded by his glory, they were beneficiaries of his goodness, yet they stopped believing what he promised. Their failure to remain faithful caused them to be prohibited from entering into their rest. They saw, but they did not enter.

They were already in the Land of Promise before they stepped foot outside Goshen, but their entrance into Canaan was contingent upon obedience. It was a reward for being faithful.

With the exception of Joshua and Caleb, that inheritance was forfeited due to disobedience and unbelief (lack of faith). God judged them because they did not esteem the inheritance he had offered; they lacked the faith that God would do what he had said, in spite of the fact that they saw his power continually.

Should they have been obedient just because they loved God? Yes. But he had promised a reward, and they did not esteem it.

By the same standard, we should be obedient because of our love for him, but we should not thumb our noses at rewards that he has promised for faithfulness. If he finds them important enough to offer, we should esteem them enough to want them.

[Numbers 14:19-23: [Moses speaking to God] Forgive the iniquity of this people according to the greatness of your steadfast love, just as you have pardoned this people, from Egypt even until now."

Then the LORD said, "I do forgive, just as you have asked; nevertheless—as I live, and as all the earth shall be filled with the glory of the LORD—none of the people who have seen my glory and the signs that I did in Egypt and in the wilderness, and yet have tested me these ten times and have not obeyed my voice, shall see the land that I swore to give to their ancestors; none of those who despised me shall see it.]

This is the example that sets our foundation for the understanding of these five warnings in Hebrews. We have been redeemed and we have been promised a reward for faithfulness. We have also been promised dire consequences for unfaithfulness.

This epistle is not written to those "Who need to get themselves saved and into the family". It is written to "holy brethren" and "partakers in the heavenly calling". Matthew 12:50 tells us the brethren are those who are doing the will of the Father. The next title are partakers, or those who are partners in the heavenly calling. This is not written to those who are outside the family. The "rest" spoken of in chapter 4:3 is not simply being born from above into the family of God it is enjoying the better inheritance that has been promised based upon faithfulness.

This is what the focus of the entire epistle has been: The future rest; the better inheritance.

This future rest requires work _**today**_!

And before you get in a huff about works and rewards (rewards are also called salvation) and how "we don't need any works", what does this passage we are studying have to say about it?

[Hebrews 4:11: Let us therefore make every effort [labor; give diligence; endeavor] to enter that rest, so that no one may fall through such disobedience [stubbornness; unfaith] as theirs [Israelites].]

With this example in mind, reflect back to our discussion about Calvinism vs Arminianism and think about the claim that many make: All those in the Exodus generation were types of unsaved people.

This is impossible.

1. The Bible states that they believed and were redeemed. They were saved, but they were not obedient.
2. All were said to be saved. Were all 600,000[32] professors and not possessors? Absurd!
3. How about Aaron and Moses? They failed to enter into the better inheritance because of unbelief. Were they professors and not possessors?

---

[32] Or, more likely, about 7,000, but either way, are all of them professors only, after having been said to have been believers?

71

4. The type that is being given is of national Israel, not individuals.[33]

We can be denied an entrance or an enjoyment of our full allotment. This is a very real warning.

We can also be rewarded positively for faithfulness. This is a very real promise.

Both the warning and the promise are centered upon our works; upon our faithfulness.

This potential loss is what the second warning is about: It is warning us against a very real potential loss.

The Third Warning: Hebrews 6:4-8

[Hebrews 6:4-8: For it is impossible to restore again to repentance those who have once been enlightened, and have tasted the heavenly gift, and have shared [been partakers] in the Holy Spirit, and have tasted the goodness of the word of God and the powers of the age to come, and then have fallen away, since on their own they are crucifying again the Son of God and are holding him up to contempt. Ground that drinks up the rain falling on it repeatedly, and that produces a crop useful to those for whom it is cultivated, receives a blessing from God. But if it produces thorns and thistles, it is worthless and on the verge of being cursed; its end is to be burned over.]

---

[33] In 1 Corinthians 10, Paul uses national Israel as a good example of bad behavior as a warning to Christians.

This is very possibly the single most controversial passage in the entire Bible.

"For it is impossible..." It is impossible to dilute this word into "difficult".[34] The subject here is simply **_impossible_**. "For mortals, it is impossible, but for God, all things are possible."[35] What is impossible? To restore again to repentance certain classes of people who have fallen away.

Why is this passage so difficult? Why is there so much controversy surrounding this passage?

This passage builds upon what has been shown in the previous two warnings, and shows us that it is very serious if a believer falls away. "Oh, but he's really a professor and not a possessor!" We have looked at that argument previously and shown that it is fallacious, but it is a very common argument in relation to this passage as well.

This passage describes not only someone who is in the family, but someone who is a faithful believer as well! The individuals described in this passage have done more than simply believed (as an event), they have been enlightened, have tasted the heavenly gift, have shared the Holy Spirit, and have tasted the goodness of the word of God and the powers of the age to come. Some of them have seen miracles and signs. Some have even been eyewitnesses of his majesty.

---

[34] Marvin Vincent.
[35] Matthew 19:26, Mark 10:27, Luke 18:27, LXX, and others.

The "age to come" is from the Greek word *aion*, and is a specific period of time. It is never "forever and ever".[36]

The individuals about whom this passage is speaking have understood the glory that awaits those who are faithful in the coming Kingdom, but have turned back to the world. They have done exactly the same thing as the Exodus generation: They have been shown the power and the glory, and instead of entering and fighting for the Land of Promise, they want to go back to Egypt. Egypt is given as a type of the world.

After Israel's faithlessness, God stated that he wanted to give all the Children of Israel the boot, except for Moses, and start over with Moses to make a great nation. Moses interceded on their behalf, and God acceded not to disinherit them entirely, but he would not change his mind about not permitting them an entrance into the better inheritance.

The next day, the children of Israel decided to repent. They changed their minds and decided to enter in on their own volition. They lost badly.

God is not frivolous. If he esteems something enough to promise it, those to whom it is promised should esteem it enough to want it. We should pay attention: The repentance in Hebrews 6:6, just as in Numbers 14, is repentance on God's part, not the believer's! Not only the type, but the grammar also supports this.

---

[36] The word "*aionian*" is often translated as "eternal", but that is an English word that does not mean the same thing today as it did in the 17th century. The English word "eternal" is from the Latin "*et ternus*" which means of great age. The word "*aionian*" can mean either "age lasting" or it can refer to the quality of the life. Most literal translations will use "age lasting" or "age abiding" or will simply transliterate it.

While there are many who think this demonstrates that a person can be unborn from above, many, if not most, think this example portrays those who are not really believers. They point to verses 7-8 to "prove" their point.

[Hebrews 6:7-8: Ground that drinks up the rain falling on it repeatedly, and that produces a crop useful to those for whom it is cultivated, receives a blessing from God. But if it produces thorns and thistles, it is worthless and on the verge of being cursed; its end is to be burned over.]

This is some strong language! "Cursed" and "burned" jumps out at them and they say, "See! Not _**really**_ believers!"

[1 Corinthians 3:12-15: Now if anyone builds on the foundation with gold, silver, precious stones, wood, hay, straw—the work of each builder will become visible, for the Day will disclose it, because it will be revealed with fire, and the fire will test what sort of work each has done. If what has been built on the foundation survives, the builder will receive a reward. If the work is burned up, the builder will suffer loss; the builder will be saved, but only as through fire.]

Believers will be judged one day. At the Judgment Seat of Christ, their works will be tried with fire. On that day, Judgment will be given, not mercy. _**Today**_ is the day for mercy and grace; that coming day is for a just recompense of reward. Jesus describes in several places both the positive and negative judgments of believers.

Do not make the mistake of relating fire and burning just to those who are unsaved.[37]

As with the first two warnings, if we fail to discern that there is more than one salvation spoken of, and if we fail to discern which one is being spoken of in this passage, we will achieve an erroneous and contradictory interpretation. The salvation of which these warnings are speaking is not the common salvation.[38]

The warnings in this passage are real possibilities. "*If* they shall fall away…" It does not say, "Although they cannot really fall away, if they should…" This is a very real possibility.

These believers have not only believed (aorist; an event), they have come into a mature knowledge (*epignosis*) of things about the Christ as the King-Priest "after the order of Melchizedek".

After coming into this mature knowledge, they fall away. They apostatize and they can never be restored to the position in which they were. This falling away reflects negatively on Jesus himself.

They were enlightened. They were illuminated.

[Hebrews 10:32: But recall those earlier days when, after you had been enlightened, you endured a hard struggle with sufferings…]

---

[37] There are two kinds of punishment: Chastisement and punitive. You chastise children.

[38] Those who try to apply this salvation to this passage must either arrive at the idea that you can become unsaved, or they are not really believers, and either position leads to contradictions and conundrums. Both views achieve what is taught in 2 Corinthians 4:4: "… the god of this world [age] has blinded the minds of the unbelievers, to keep them from seeing the light of the gospel of the glory of Christ, who is the image of God."

[Luke 11:34-36: Your eye is the lamp of your body. If your eye is healthy, your whole body is full of light; but if it is not healthy, your body is full of darkness. Therefore consider whether the light in you is not darkness. If then your whole body is full of light, with no part of it in darkness, it will be as full of light [illuminated] as when a lamp gives you light with its rays."]

Beware of what you look upon, it can make you sick if you are looking in the wrong places.

[John 1:9: The true light, which enlightens [illuminates] everyone, was coming into the world.]

The natural (soulish) man cannot be illuminated in spiritual things, neither does the soulish man share in the Holy Spirit or partake in spiritual gifts.

[1 Corinthians 2:14: Those who are unspiritual [natural; soulish] do not receive the gifts of God's Spirit, for they are foolishness to them, and they are unable to understand them because they are spiritually discerned.]

These are things that are the "meat" (solid food) of the Word. A baby needs milk and cannot consume solid food; someone who is not yet born certainly has no part with solid food.

[Hebrews 5:12-14: For though by this time you ought to be teachers, you need someone to teach you again the basic elements of the oracles of God. You need milk, not solid food; for everyone who lives on milk, being still an infant, is unskilled in the word of righteousness. But solid food is for the mature, for those whose faculties have been trained by practice to distinguish good from evil.]

These individuals have tasted of the Heavenly gift. It is **_the_** gift; singular. This is not our common salvation. Hebrews 6:3 says, "And we will do this if God permits". Jesus died for all, so any person who accepts that free offer would obviously be permitted to be saved. But a gift can be taken back. The context is the gift of the Land Flowing with Milk and Honey as a type, so the antitype also portrays a gift that can be taken back. A good example is in Matthew 19 in which a servant was given a gift of being freed from debt, but that gift was rescinded because of the servant's behavior. Romans 5:15 tells us that **_the_** gift was offered to the many, not to all. All can enter into the family. He died that all men might be saved. The common salvation is not restricted to the many. Romans 6:22-23 tells us that **_the_** gift is *aionian* life, which is life in the age to come. [YLT Romans 6:23: for the wages of the sin *is* death, and the gift of God *is* life age-during in Christ Jesus our Lord.]

[Hebrews 2:9: but we do see Jesus, who for a little while was made lower than the angels, now crowned with glory and honor because of the suffering of death, so that by the grace of God he might taste death for everyone.]

Jesus did not just sort of die, he **_died_** on the cross. He tasted death. Those who have tasted the heavenly gift were not simply sort of participating in a passing thing, they have a complete knowledge of it, just as the Children of Israel had tasted of the fruit of the land brought back by the spies.

Those being spoken of are partakers in the Holy Spirit. This word "partakers" can be translated as "fellows" or "comrades" or "partners". This word is used to describe the co-heirs with Jesus, not just some outsider who just happened to sort of be there, but was not really there.

The Children of Israel at Kadesh-Barnea had the words of God on tablets of stone, God dwelt in their midst, the spies had told them how great the land was, and they tasted the fruits thereof. They were ready to enter the land and obtain their inheritance as the firstborn of God. They had a mature knowledge (*epignosis*). Yet they fell away and found it impossible to be renewed again unto repentance.

This warning passage is referring to true believers who have *epignosis* of these things.

Yet there is the very real possibility they can fall away.

If they fall away, it is impossible to restore them again to repentance.

This is not easy. The spies told everyone that it was a land flowing with milk and honey, but they also brought back reports about the difficulties involved with taking the land, and they concentrated on the difficulties. There were Nephilim, and they lived in walled cities, and it will be hard, and it was really scary. "We can't go up against them; they are too great for us."

But two of the spies, Joshua and Caleb said, "We can do it!"

As was typical, the Children of Israel listened to both, then wept and murmured, had no faith in spite of everything they had seen, and looked back to Egypt. They went so far as to start back.

79

They fell away.

The Children of Israel turned their backs on God so God turned his back on them. None, except Joshua and Caleb, entered into the Land.[39]

There was no renewal again unto repentance that was possible because they had brought shame to the name of God, who was dwelling in their midst, because they did not believe his promise that he would lead them to victory.

"Repentance" is a change of mind and in both the type and the antitype, the repentance is God's.

The Children of Israel repented; they decided to go into the Land anyway. But God did not repent.

This is what the warning in Hebrews 6 is about. If a believer comes into *epignosis* of things to come, and that believer becomes apostate, he will be cut off from the better part of his inheritance, just as the apostate Israelites were cut off. He will not be "restored again to repentance".

He will not become unsaved, but he will not ***enter***. He will fail to obtain the better inheritance.

"Well, doesn't that seem a bit extreme?" No. An apostate brings shame and reproach upon the name of Christ. He does not believe God's promises. He is, "Crucifying again the Son of God and holding him up to contempt".

---

[39] I can imagine the thoughts going through Joshua's and Caleb's heads, thinking, "You dummies!"

"Well, then, he's obviously a professor and not a possessor!" Stop that thought right now!

In order for a believer to fall away, he would have to first come into a mature knowledge and understanding of things concerning the coming age, and then fall away from that. He must have his eye on the Kingdom and then turn back to Egypt, which is a type of the world, and the god of this world is Satan. You cannot fall away from somewhere you have never been. If you want to skydive, you cannot fall away from the plane unless you are first on the plane.

You have free will. God will allow you to fall away. But at a certain point, he will not allow you to return.

The Fourth Warning: Hebrews 10:26-39

[Hebrews 10:26-39: For if we willfully persist in sin after having received the knowledge of the truth, there no longer remains a sacrifice for sins, but a fearful prospect of judgment, and a fury of fire that will consume the adversaries. Anyone who has violated the Law of Moses dies without mercy "on the testimony of two or three witnesses." How much worse punishment do you think will be deserved by those who have spurned the Son of God, profaned the blood of the covenant by which they were sanctified, and outraged the Spirit of grace? For we know the one who said, "Vengeance is mine, I will repay." And again, "The Lord will judge his people." It is a fearful thing to fall into the hands of the living God.

But recall those earlier days when, after you had been enlightened, you endured a hard struggle with sufferings, sometimes being publicly exposed to abuse and persecution, and sometimes being partners with those so treated. For you had compassion for those who were in prison, and you cheerfully accepted the plundering of your possessions, knowing that you yourselves possessed something better and more lasting. Do not, therefore, abandon that confidence of yours; it brings a great reward. For you need endurance, so that when you have done the will of God, you may receive what was promised.

For yet "in a very little while, the one who is coming will come and will not delay; but my righteous one will live by faith. My soul takes no pleasure in anyone who shrinks back." But we are not among those who shrink back and so are lost [*apollumi*], but among those who have faith and so are saved [obtain acquisition of life].]

We are now at the fourth warning in Hebrews, and the trend has continued so that this warning is more severe than the ones preceding it and it builds upon the previous warnings. This warning talks about willful sin (lawlessness; doing what is right in one's own eyes), a fury or fierceness of fire, and a more severe punishment (vengeance; retributive punishment, not chastisement).

Verse 25 uses the phrase, "As you see the day approaching" to segue into this warning. The "day" that is approaching is a reference to events that will take place in the end times. These events concern the Judgment Seat of Christ and the Millennial Kingdom, both of which are the focus of the entire book of Hebrews.

We have looked briefly at willful sin in the past. Those who commit willful sin after receiving knowledge of the truth will face a much harsher judgment.

In order to help us understand this passage, we will look at some of the words in it.

"We": This warning includes the writer along with those to whom he is writing. These are not those who are "professors not possessors". This warning is to those who are in the family and have been weaned from the milk. Verse 29 tells us they have been sanctified. In verse 23, they are told to "hold fast". Just as you cannot fall away from a plane you have not been on, you cannot hold fast onto something which you do not have hold.

"Sin": It is correctly "persist in sin" as it is translated here. It is a present, active, plural, participle. "If we continually persist in sinning."

"Willfully": Voluntarily or by choice because you believe you have the right to do it. One who practices willful sin says, "I have the right to do this because…", and then proceeds to justify the behavior in his own eyes. Willful sin is lawlessness.[40]

"After": This is after they have received the knowledge of truth. These are not babes in the Word, they are mature believers. They have been weaned from the milk and have been dining on steak and potatoes.

[Hebrews 5:13-14: for everyone who lives on milk, being still an infant, is unskilled in the word of righteousness. But solid food is for the mature, for those whose faculties have been trained by practice to distinguish good from evil.]

---

[40] Some translations translate lawlessness as "iniquity". All lawlessness is sin, but lawlessness is treated much more harshly because it is embraced and practiced heartily and without repentance. Sin is simply missing the mark.

"Knowledge": This is *epignosis*. As we saw at the beginning of this study, this is a deeper knowledge; it is knowledge upon knowledge.

"***The*** Truth": There are three areas under consideration that are more than simply milk: The Son of God, the blood of the covenant, and the Spirit of grace. We often teach that grace is "unmerited favor", but throughout the NT, grace is defined as "the power of Christ".

[Revelation 21:7: Those who conquer [he who overcomes, singular; this is the spirit of grace in action] will inherit [blood of the covenant] these things, and I will be ~~their~~ his God and ~~they~~ he will be my ~~children~~ son [singular; son of God][41].]

The word "Son in this passage is singular. Sonship is a position of maturity. We are already children of God, but we can become sons.

The deeper knowledge of the truth is like salt; it brings savor to meat. Salt, as a seasoning, is not the origin of the flavor, but it enhances the flavor. In the case of the aromatic salts referred to in Matthew 5:13, the salt is not the origin of the aroma, but it enhances the aroma. Our sense of taste is strongly related to our sense of smell.

[Matthew 5:13: "You are the salt of the earth; but if salt has lost its taste, how can its saltiness be restored? It is no longer good for anything, but is thrown out and trampled under foot."][42]

---

[41] See the study on "Sons or Children".

[42] Salt here probably does not refer to what we are used to as table salt, but is most likely an aromatic chemical salt that was used in sacrifices to create an

"Trampled" in Matthew 5:13 is the same word that is found in our current passage in Hebrews 10:29, which says, "How much worse punishment do you think will be deserved by those who have ~~spurned~~ trampled the Son of God…"

When a child of God lives in lawlessness, he does not esteem being an overcomer, he does not esteem having an inheritance, and he does not esteem one day being proclaimed as a son of God; these things become so low in his estimation that he tramples them underfoot.

"No longer remains a sacrifice for sin": Under the Law of Moses, there were some sins that could be forgiven by sacrifice or offering, and there were others that required the death penalty. The presumptuous sin in Numbers 15:30 required the death penalty. "Presumptuous" means high-handed or defiant, and is the same thing as the sin of lawlessness. There was not a sacrifice or offering that could be offered to restore that individual back to fellowship. When Eli the priest honored his sons more than he honored the Lord, it was judged that the sin would not be purged with sacrifice or offering forever.

[Hebrews 9:22: Indeed, under the law ***almost everything*** is purified with blood, and without the shedding of blood there is no forgiveness of sins.]

"Almost everything" means there are some things that are not purified with blood. Not all the sins of the children of God will be forgiven until after there is a new heaven and a new Earth.

---

aromatic incense. It is kept in a box, and if it becomes wet, it no longer works for its purpose and is thrown on the slick, wet steps for traction, and is literally trodden under foot.

[Matthew 12:32: Whoever speaks a word against the Son of Man will be forgiven, but whoever speaks against the Holy Spirit will not be forgiven, either in this age or in the age to come.]

"Worse punishment": Under the Law of Moses, those who sinned presumptuously were sentenced to a physical death. However, under the New Testament, we are not to fear a physical death.

[Proverbs 13:13: Those who despise the word bring destruction on themselves, but those who respect the commandment will be rewarded.]

While we are not to fear physical death in this age, we should fear destruction in the age to come.

[Matthew 16:25, 27: For those who want to save their life will lose it [*apollumi*; future], and those who lose their life for my sake will find it…"For the Son of Man is to come with his angels in the glory of his Father, and then he will ***repay*** everyone for ***what has been done*** [his works]".]

As we can see, this warning is not to those who are babies; it is not for someone who simply has a casual knowledge of the things of the Lord. This warning is given to those who are mature believers and have a full knowledge; they have a mature understanding of the hope of glory in the coming age. If we turn back – if we do not esteem the things that have been offered – that is a direct insult in the face of God.

Have you ever given a gift to someone that you put a lot of thought into and esteemed highly just to have them ignore it or despise it? How did that make you feel? That is what happens when one turns back, it is despising what God has offered. Hence, those who willfully forsake him will receive a much more severe judgment.

Do you really want to stand at the Judgment Seat after having trampled under foot the Son of God, profaned the blood of the covenant, or outraged the spirit of grace?

[2 Corinthians 5:9-11: So whether we are at home or away, we make it our aim to please him. For all of us must appear before the judgment seat of Christ, so that each may receive recompense for what has been done in the body, whether good or evil. Therefore, knowing the fear [terror] of the Lord, we try to persuade others; but we ourselves are well known to God, and I hope that we are also well known to your consciences.]

How does God judge unfaithful servants?

[Matthew 25:26-30: But his master replied, 'You wicked and lazy slave! You knew, did you, that I reap where I did not sow, and gather where I did not scatter? Then you ought to have invested my money with the bankers, and on my return I would have received what was my own with interest. So take the talent from him, and give it to the one with the ten talents. For to all those who have, more will be given, and they will have an abundance; but from those who have nothing, even what they have will be taken away. As for this worthless slave, throw him into the outer darkness, where there will be weeping and gnashing of teeth.']

That is pretty severe!

"Outer darkness" describes a place of great sorrow in which an unfaithful servant experiences grief. It is based upon the works of the servant. There are potential negative aspects of the Judgment Seat of Christ. Rewards are what you have earned. Some receive "good stuff" while others receive lashes and outer darkness.

Those who are cast into outer darkness have forfeited their inheritance. Those who are lawless will be denied an entrance into the Kingdom of the Heavens.

[Matthew 7:21-23: "Not everyone who says to me, 'Lord, Lord,' will enter the kingdom of heaven, but only the one who does the will of my Father in heaven. On that day many will say to me, 'Lord, Lord, did we not prophesy in your name, and cast out demons in your name, and do many deeds of power in your name?' Then I will declare to them, 'I never knew you; go away from me, you evildoers [workers of lawlessness].']

When they said, "Did we not do all these great works in your name?" he does not reply, "No, you didn't!" He tells them they were lawless. They did what was right in their own eyes. They may have performed many good works, but they were not works of faith.

[1 Corinthians 12:3: Therefore I want you to understand that no one speaking by the Spirit of God ever says "Let Jesus be cursed!" and no one can say "Jesus is Lord" except by the Holy Spirit.]

These people are in the family (they called him "Lord"), but they are not doing what they are supposed to be doing. They will suffer loss, but will be saved, only as through fire, as we are told in 1 Corinthians 3:15.

Those who do the will of the Father are being obedient, not lawless. How can we be obedient? How do we serve him acceptably?

[Hebrews 12:28: Therefore, since we are receiving a kingdom that cannot be shaken, let us ~~give thanks~~ have grace[43], by which we offer to God an acceptable worship with reverence and awe.]

[Romans 5:2: through whom we have obtained access [by faith] to this grace in which we stand; and we boast in our hope of sharing the glory of God.]

We access grace by faith. Faith is a lifestyle. Lifestyle is works.

[Hebrews 11:6-7: And ***without faith it is impossible to please God***, for whoever would approach him must believe that he exists and that he rewards those who seek him. By faith Noah, warned by God about events as yet unseen, respected the warning and built an ark to save his household; by this he condemned the

---

[43] The NRSV chose to translate this as "give thanks". The word "*charin*" could be either "thanks" or "grace" (or a few other shades of meaning such as "favor" or "goodwill"). However, "grace" seems to make more sense, and if "thanks" is the correct word, it would be "let us ***have*** thanks". Luke 2:40, speaking of Jesus says "the grace of God was upon him". Acts 14:26 says they were "commended to the grace of God for the work they had completed". In Acts 15:40, the believers commended the grace of the Lord to Paul. Romans 3:24 says "they are now justified by his grace as a gift." Since the grace of God is the power of Christ (2 Corinthians 12:9), "grace" makes much more sense in Hebrews 12:28. Different translations translate this verse in different ways.

world and became an heir to the righteousness that is in accordance with faith.]

If we are faithful, we will be rewarded. If we are unfaithful, we will also be rewarded. Those rewards will not be equal rewards.

If we trample the Son under foot; if we profane the blood of the covenant; if we outrage the spirit of grace… Look out!

The Fifth Warning: Hebrews 12:25-29

[Hebrews 12:25-29: See that you do not refuse the one who is speaking; for if they did not escape when they refused the one who warned them on earth, how much less will we escape if we reject the one who warns from heaven! At that time his voice shook the earth; but now he has promised, "Yet once more I will shake not only the earth but also the heaven." This phrase, "Yet once more," indicates the removal of what is shaken—that is, created things—so that what cannot be shaken may remain. Therefore, since we are receiving a kingdom that cannot be shaken, let us give thanks have grace [keep having grace], by which we offer to God an acceptable worship with reverence and awe; for indeed our God is a consuming fire.]

Many people like to study the "great faith" chapter.

[Hebrews 11:1-3: Now faith is the assurance of things hoped for, the conviction of things not seen. Indeed, by faith our ancestors received approval. By faith we understand that the worlds were prepared by the word of God, so that what is seen was made from things that are not visible.]

To summarize the rest of the "great faith" chapter: By faith Abel offered to God a more acceptable sacrifice than Cain's...by faith Enoch was taken so that he did not experience death...without faith it is impossible to please God...by faith Noah...by faith Abraham...by faith Sarah...by faith Isaac...by faith Jacob...by faith Joseph...by faith Moses...by faith the people passed through the Red Sea...by faith the walls of Jericho fell...by faith Rahab...Gideon, Barak, Samson, Jephthah, of David and Samuel and the prophets...women received their dead, others were tortured, others suffered mocking and flogging, and even chains and imprisonment...stoned to death, sawn in two, killed by the sword; they went about in skins of sheep and goats, destitute, persecuted, tormented...they wandered in deserts and mountains, and in caves and holes in the ground...these are all commended for their faith.

We are shown all these great examples of faith, yet they have not yet received the promise.

[Hebrews 11:40: since God had provided something better so that they would not, apart from us, be made perfect.]

We do not have some sort of merit that makes us better than they were, but we are now in the age of grace.

Many people study this "great faith" chapter, and go on into chapter 12 and see the discussion on running the race with patience.

[Hebrews 12:1-2: Therefore, since we are surrounded by so great a cloud of witnesses, let us also lay aside every weight and the sin that clings so closely [easily distracts], and let us run with perseverance the race that is set before us, looking to Jesus the pioneer and perfecter of our faith, who for the sake of the joy that was set before him endured the cross, disregarding its shame, and has taken his seat at the right hand of the throne of God.]

There! Now don't you feel just great! This is a passage that many people like because it is a feel-good chapter. You can raise your hands in praise, sway to the music and shout, then go home feeling great… and you *__should__* feel great.

But you should not stop reading there.

[Hebrews 12:3-15: Consider him who endured such hostility against himself from sinners, so that you may not grow weary or lose heart. In your struggle against sin you have not yet resisted to the point of shedding your blood. And you have forgotten the exhortation that addresses you as children—"My child, do not regard lightly the discipline of the Lord, or lose heart when you are punished by him; for the Lord disciplines those whom he loves, and chastises every child whom he accepts."

Endure trials for the sake of discipline. God is treating you as children; for what child is there whom a parent does not discipline? If you do not have that discipline in which all children share, then you are illegitimate and not his children. Moreover, we had human parents to discipline us, and we respected them. Should we not be even more willing to be subject to the Father of spirits and live? For they disciplined us for a short time as seemed best to them, but he disciplines us for our good, in order that we may share his holiness. Now, discipline always seems painful rather than pleasant at the time, but later it yields the peaceful fruit of righteousness to those who have been trained by it.

Therefore lift your drooping hands and strengthen your weak knees, and make straight paths for your feet, so that what is lame may not be put out of joint, but rather be healed.

Pursue peace with everyone, and the holiness without which no one will see the Lord. See to it that no one fails to obtain the grace of God; that no root of bitterness springs up and causes trouble, and through it many become defiled.]

This part of the chapter is not nearly as popular as the earlier part. Discussing chastisement makes many people uncomfortable because they want to hear that there is no accountability for their behavior. Others like to use it as a threat of getting kicked out of the family. Most like to simply apply this to someone else.

Chastising and punitive punishments are not the same thing.

Chastisement carries with it the idea of child training and not merely punishment for doing wrong. It is the rod of correction, and society today is told that it is simply wrong to chastise your child. In many places it is now against the law to chastise your child and we see where that is leading. People do not like to hear that their behavior is not fine and dandy; they simply want verification that nothing is wrong with their behavior so they can go home and feel good.

Those who make it this far in the passage really do not like to go onto the next section.

[Hebrews 12:16-17: See to it that no one becomes like Esau, an immoral and godless person, who sold his birthright for a single meal. You know that later, when he wanted to inherit the blessing, he was rejected, for he found no chance to repent [change his father's mind], even though he sought the blessing with tears.]

This passage is used to introduce the fifth warning in the book of Hebrews.

This makes many people very uncomfortable. It shakes the faith of some who believe in the security of the believer, so they try to avoid it or rationalize it out, and others use it to show that you earn your salvation, and yet others simply throw their hands up in the air, declare it to be a mystery, then return to chapter 11 so they can feel good again.

There is no story throughout human history that is more tragic than the story of Esau. Esau, as the firstborn son, had it all: His portion of the inheritance was the double portion and the birthright. Esau would get the Ferrari and Jacob would get the Yugo.

The birthright is the sum of all the advantages that accrued to the eldest son. These were not definitely set in stone in patriarchal times, but great respect was paid to the firstborn in the household, and as the family widened into a tribe, this grew into a sustained authority, which was undefined except by custom.

[Numbers 7:1-2: On the day when Moses had finished setting up the tabernacle, and had anointed and consecrated it with all its furnishings, and had anointed and consecrated the altar with all its utensils, the leaders of Israel, heads of their ancestral houses, the leaders of the tribes, who were over those who were enrolled, made offerings.]

Over time, the rights of the eldest son came to be more definite:

1. The functions of the priesthood in the family with the paternal blessing.
2. A "double portion" of the paternal property was allotted by the Mosaic Law.
3. The eldest son succeeded to the official authority of the father. The first-born of the king was his successor by law.

In all these Jesus was the firstborn of the Father. The birthright is not something to be lightly esteemed. It is something upon which we should place a high value.

Esau is a lesson for all of us.[44] Jacob and Esau were opposites.

[Genesis 25:27: When the boys grew up, Esau was a skillful hunter, a man of the field, while Jacob was a quiet man, living in tents.]

Jacob was a pious man who found pleasure in the quiet life of home.

Esau was a man of action! He was a skillful hunter and a man of the field. He would be highly praised in the modern world.

[Matthew 13:38a: the field is the world...]

Esau was a man of the world.

---

[44] We are told that Esau was hairy. The name "Esau" probably means "robust", but the word "hairy" is from a word that can also be translated as "kid" (goat). Numbers 18:17 tells us that goats are holy animals, so they are not a type of the unsaved, but they are headstrong, stubborn, and an all-around pain to deal with.

One day, Esau came in from hunting, he was famished, and he sold his birthright for a bowl of soup.

Did you ever stop to wonder why Esau sold his birthright for a bowl of soup? I mean, come on! A side of mutton with a side of potatoes and carrots, maybe, but soup? He states that he is at the point of death. Why? Could he not make a sandwich or something?

[Genesis 25:32: Esau said, "I am about to die; of what use is a birthright to me?"]

"I'm so hungry I'm about to die" is a saying we have all probably said. But we all knew that it was hyperbole. We did not mean it.

What is the backstory? If you read the background history that contemporary Jewish society would have been familiar with, we know that when Esau went out hunting, he was hunting Nimrod. Mainly because Nimrod was hunting him, but Esau was successful in that hunt and Nimrod's men were coming after him. He did not have enough faith in God to protect him and he felt that his birthright would not be any good, so he made a contract to sell his birthright to his brother and that bowl of soup sealed the contract. (Esau also desired to rule the world and stole Nimrod's clothing which was the clothing God had made for Adam. If Esau had been successful in ruling the world, he would have had no need for his birthright, therefore he despised it on two counts.)

There is also more to the saga of Jacob and Esau that gives much insight into the few sentences the Bible gives. Context is everything, therefore it is important to know the context of statements.[45]

Jacob, who was pious, esteemed the birthright. Esau, a man of the world, did not.

Esau did not look to the future; his mind was in the present world. He disdained the birthright.

Later, digging his hole a little deeper, he enlarged his unrighteousness by marrying not one, but two Philistine women.[46]

After continuing his life of unrighteousness, he is still expecting to receive the blessing, even though he had forfeited the birthright. Isaac is even planning on giving it to him. But Jacob gets that as well.

Since the hole is not yet deep enough, Esau proceeds to dig it yet a little deeper, and marries another wife. This time it is a daughter of Ishmael.

Every time, Esau, a man of action (works), being a man of the world, turned to the ways of the world and to his own understanding in order to please his father. By failing to take spiritual things into account, he departed from righteousness. We need to understand that we cannot achieve righteousness through the ways of the world or through our own understanding. There are plenty of "good" people who are doing good things who will be in big trouble one day!

---

[45] In this case, the context is the book of Jasher, with which the Jews would have been familiar, not as Scripture, but as history.
[46] I bet that Christmas dinner was interesting!

Esau was a worldly man. What happens when you live for this world?

[Galatians 6:7-8: Do not be deceived; God is not mocked, for you reap whatever you sow. If you sow to your own flesh, you will reap corruption from the flesh; but if you sow to the Spirit, you will reap eternal *life* from the Spirit.]

If we live for the world as Esau did, we are in danger of losing our better inheritance. If we live in the Spirit, we can gain the birthright of the firstborn.

If we despise the birthright we will live a life of physical gratification. If we esteem the birthright we will desire to live a life of righteousness.

Esau, as the firstborn son, was in line to enjoy the rights and privileges of the firstborn son: Priesthood of the family, kingship, and a double portion of the inheritance. He did not esteem these things. He did not consider them important until it was too late.

Esau was not kicked out of the family. We seem him at family gatherings later in the Bible. He still received an inheritance and a blessing. But it was not the inheritance and blessing that was the birthright of the firstborn; it was not the better inheritance.

When he realized the importance of the birthright of the firstborn, he begged and pleaded for Isaac to change his mind and bless him. He could not change his father's mind "even though he sought the blessing with tears". Their father could not and would not change his mind because the blessing had already been given to Jacob.

That is the basis for this fifth, and most drastic, warning in the book of Hebrews. We are admonished to esteem spiritual things and not forfeit our birthright because of the things of the world. We can lose out.

This warning tells us to pay attention! Do not refuse God about these blessings! Those to whom this epistle is written were in real danger of losing out because they were shutting their ears to the voice of God. That is what those in the wilderness did that are being spoken of in Hebrews 12:19.

[Hebrews 12:19b: "…and a voice whose words made the hearers beg that not another word be spoken to them."]

The word that is translated here as "beg" is a word that implies a refusal, and not a request. In other words, the hearers were not going to listen to another word from God directly. If we are unwilling to listen, just as they were unwilling to listen, there will be dire consequences!

This is referring back to Exodus 19 and 20 in which the children of Israel chose not to speak to God directly; they asked Moses to do it for them; they demanded he act as an intercessor. This is not what God wanted! God wanted a nation of priests and kings.

[Exodus 19:5-6a: Now therefore, if you obey my voice and keep my covenant, you shall be my treasured possession out of all the peoples. Indeed, the whole earth is mine, but you shall be for me a priestly kingdom [kingdom of priests] and a holy nation.]

We are given the type of the Exodus generation and their shortcomings and failures as a warning against our potential shortcomings and failures.

[1 Corinthians 10:11: These things happened to them to serve as an example, and they were written down to instruct us, on whom the ends of the ages have come.]

In modern pop-psychology, this is simply emanating complete and total negativity. But this is a warning against bad behavior, so we will know how to properly behave ourselves. If the Exodus generation feared his voice, then when we hear his voice – when we listen to what he says – we must have grace so that we can serve him with reverence and awe.

One day we ***will be*** judged. Throughout the book of Hebrews, and indeed, throughout the entire Bible, we are reminded that there is judgment coming. Right now, we have the opportunity to judge ourselves; one day, it will be too late. It behooves us greatly to remember, "Indeed, our God is a consuming fire."[47]

There is a coming Millennial Kingdom, and we can simply see it or we can enter in and possess it; we can enjoy our full allotment and rule and reign as co-heirs with Jesus, if we stand firm and do not make shipwreck of the faith. The coming Kingdom is the central focus of the book of Hebrews, and we are admonished throughout to persevere so we will not forfeit our inheritance (our rewards), and we are warned about what will happen if we are not faithful.[48]

---

[47] Hebrews 12:29.
[48] See Hebrews 1:9, 1:13-14, 4:1-11, 6:9, 10:25, 10:37-38, and 12:28.

This is all about working and persevering. Our Works will be judged at the Judgment Seat of Christ and will determine whether we receive "good stuff" or if we are "saved, but only as through fire".

The Kingdom is future, but we can receive the Kingdom now, by putting ourselves in the camp of the Lord and laying up treasure in heaven.

[Matthew 6:19-21: "Do not store up for yourselves treasures on earth, where moth and rust consume and where thieves break in and steal; but store up for yourselves treasures in heaven, where neither moth nor rust consumes and where thieves do not break in and steal. For where your treasure is, there your heart will be also.]

We are given as a type, the story of David and Saul. After David was anointed king, he did not ascend the throne immediately. Saul still reigned. But those who allied themselves with David were rewarded greatly when he came into his kingdom.

Currently, Satan still rules on the Earth,[49] but we can ally ourselves with the Lord, and when he comes into his Kingdom (when he ascends to the throne), we will be rewarded for faithful service. If we ally ourselves with the Enemy, we will also be appropriately rewarded for that service.

"Oh, you're so negative! God loves you!" Yes, God loves me, and he loves you. He loves you so much that he provided a way for you to be faithful. We are encouraged to persevere, and the warnings against apostasy serve as something with which to compare the "good stuff" to the "bad stuff". We are warned about

---

[49] Ephesians 2:2, John 16:11, 2 Corinthians 4:4.

the consequences, so we may better appreciate the positive rewards.

"Don't touch the hot stove!" is a negative command, but it has a positive effect if you heed the warning.

Throughout the book of Hebrews, with all the severe warnings, there are also encouragements, like a coach cheering from the sidelines.

[Hebrews 6:1a: Therefore let us go on toward perfection [maturity]...]

[Hebrews 10:23a: Let us hold fast to the confession of our hope without wavering...]

[Hebrews 10:35: Do not, therefore, abandon that confidence of yours; it brings a great reward.]

[Hebrews 12:1b: ...let us run with perseverance the race that is set before us.]

Although there are many places with admonishments, they are followed by encouragements and reminders about the good service already done and the rewards for faithful service. He tells us that our suffering will not be in vain.

[Philippians 2:5-11: Let the same mind be in you that was in Christ Jesus, who, though he was in the form of God, did not regard equality with God as something to be exploited, but emptied himself, taking the form of a slave, being born in human likeness. And being found in human form, he humbled himself and became obedient to the point of death— even death on a cross.

Therefore God also highly exalted him and gave him the name that is above every name, so that at the name of Jesus every knee should bend, in heaven and on earth and under the earth, and every tongue should confess that Jesus Christ is Lord, to the glory of God the Father.]

We are encouraged to seek a similar position. We do that by running a good race or by fighting the good fight. We have to keep our eyes focused on the things of the Lord, and in order to do that we must look through the lens of the Scriptures.

[Colossians 3:1-4: So if you have been raised with Christ, seek the things that are above, where Christ is, seated at the right hand of God. Set your minds on things that are above, not on things that are on earth, for you have died, and your life is hidden with Christ in God. When Christ who is your life is revealed, then you also will be revealed with him in glory.]

[Colossians 1:26-27: the mystery that has been hidden throughout the ages and generations but has now been revealed to his saints. To them God chose to make known how great among the Gentiles are the riches of the glory of this mystery, which is Christ in you, the hope of glory.]

These warnings we have been studying are the way that God is guiding us to "be conformed to the image of his Son, in order that he might be the firstborn within a large family [among many brothers.]"[50]

---

[50] Romans 8:29.

We can lose much. If we want the better inheritance, we need to move on to perfection. If we want the reward of the firstborn, we need to grow up and realize we are accountable for our behavior.

[Hebrews 6:1-2: Therefore let us go on toward perfection [maturity],[51] leaving behind the basic teaching about Christ, and not laying again the foundation: repentance from dead works and faith toward God, instruction about baptisms, laying on of hands, resurrection of the dead, and eternal judgment.]

As we saw back at the beginning of this study, man is a three part being, and salvation, as it concerns us as individuals, is a three part salvation.

[1 Thessalonians 5:23: May [optative; probable failure] the God of peace himself sanctify you entirely; and may [optative] your spirit *and* soul *and* body be kept sound [complete] and blameless at the coming of our Lord Jesus Christ.]

The Bible teaches us that man is a spirit *and* a soul *and* a body. The teaching of natural evolution holds that man, being merely an animal, is only a body and a soul *or* spirit (life force).

[Hebrews 4:12: Indeed, the word of God is living and active, sharper than any two-edged sword, piercing until it divides *soul*

---

[51] In the Bible, the word "perfect" should not be used in the modern American sense of "entirely without flaws, defects, or shortcomings", but should be used in the sense of the origins of the word which means "maturity" as the footnote in the NRSV says or "finished, complete, ready" or "to bring to full development". It is from the word *teleios*, and the phrase literally means, "Carried on to completeness". It is in contrast to the stage of elementary knowledge in "leaving behind the basic teaching about Christ, and not laying again the foundation". See the previous verse (Hebrews 5:14) in which we are told that "solid food is for the mature".

**from spirit**, joints from marrow; it is able to judge the thoughts and intentions of the heart.]

Remember, while God judges intentions, direction, not intention, determines the destination.

The word "salvation" is not always referring to the same thing. We cannot lose our common (spiritual) salvation, but we do stand in danger of losing our position in the coming Kingdom, which is also called "salvation" (salvation of the soul). We can fall short. Hope is not a guarantee. In Acts 24:26, Felix hoped that Paul would give him money, but he did not. In Luke 23:8, Herod hoped to see some miracle from Jesus, but he did not. Neither of these hopes were fulfilled. Our hope is that we remain faithful so we may receive glory as he has promised for those who remain faithful, but we may fail. Our hope is to endure to the end.

It is time to wake up and pay attention! Every individual has the opportunity to judge himself in this age, but judgment by Christ awaits every individual within the family of God at the Judgment Seat of Christ. The "so great salvation" spoken of in Hebrews 2:3 awaits those who finish the course; those who serve him faithfully; those who stand firm; those who persist in righteousness. Our hope is not to get to heaven, but to hear "well done".

Heed the five warnings in this epistle and one day you may hear "well done" and you will "enter into the joy of the Lord".

Adoption

[Romans 9:1-5: I am speaking the truth in Christ—I am not lying; my conscience confirms it by the Holy Spirit – I have great sorrow and unceasing anguish in my heart. For I could wish that I myself were accursed and cut off from Christ for the sake of my ~~own people~~ [brethren], my kindred according to the *__flesh__*. They are Israelites, and to them belong the adoption [*huiothesia*], the glory, the covenants, the giving of the law, the worship, and the promises; to them belong the patriarchs, and from them, according to the flesh [talking about his humanity; emphasizing family], comes the Messiah, who is over all, God blessed forever. Amen.]

"They are Israelites, and to them belong *__the adoption__*, the glory, the covenants, the giving of the law, the worship, and the promises." Several definite articles in this sentence. Today, we are going to concentrate on the first item in this list.

[Deuteronomy 7:6-7: For you are a people holy [*__holy people__*] to the LORD your God; the LORD your God has *__chosen__* you out of all the peoples on earth to be *__his people__*, his treasured possession. It was not because you were more numerous than any other people that the LORD set his heart on you and chose you—for *__you were the fewest__* of all peoples.]

[Deuteronomy 14:2: For you are a people holy to the LORD your God; it is *__you__* the LORD has *__chosen__* out of all the peoples on earth to be his people, *__his treasured possession__*.]

[Deuteronomy 28:9-10: The LORD will establish you as *__his__* holy people, as he has sworn to you, if you keep the commandments of the LORD your God and walk in his ways. All the peoples of the earth shall see that you are called by the name of the LORD, and they shall be afraid of you.]

[Deuteronomy 28:13: The LORD will make you _**the head**_, and not the tail; you shall be only _**at the top**_, and _**not at the bottom**_—_**if you obey**_ the commandments of the LORD your God, which I am commanding you today, by diligently observing them...]

_**If**_ you obey. Some promises that are given by God are unconditional. These promises in this passage are conditional, and they are conditioned upon being faithful.

[Matthew 21:42-43: Jesus said to them, "Have you never read in the scriptures: 'The stone that the builders rejected has become the cornerstone; this was the Lord's doing, and it is amazing in our eyes'? Therefore I tell you, the kingdom of God will be taken away from you and given to a people that produces the fruits of the kingdom.]

A peach tree is still a peach tree, even if it is barren of fruit. These people are still _**his**_ people, but if they do not produce fruits of the Kingdom, they will lose reward.

[1 Peter 2:8-10: "A stone that makes them [Isreal] stumble, and a rock that makes them fall." They stumble because they disobey the word, as they were destined to do. But you [the Gentile church] are a _**chosen**_ [elect] race, a royal priesthood, a holy nation, God's own people [people for his possession], in order that you may proclaim the mighty acts of him who _**called you**_ out of darkness into his marvelous light. Once you _**were not a people, but now you are God's people**_; once you had not received mercy, but _**now**_ you have received mercy.]

They were not a people, but now they are *__the__* people. They are God's people, with a purpose.

[Ephesians 3:5-6: In former generations this mystery was not made known to humankind, as it has now been revealed to his holy apostles and prophets by the Spirit: that is, the *__Gentiles have become fellow heirs__*, members of the same body, and sharers in the promise in Christ Jesus through the gospel.]

Gentiles have always been able to be in the family of God. Rahab, the harlot of Jericho, was a Gentile, and she was part of the lineage of Jesus. Nineveh was a Gentile city, and they were saved through the preaching of Jonah. Gentiles were not promised a heavenly inheritance, but they were promised an earthly inheritance. That has changed.

[Ezekiel 47:22: You shall allot it as an inheritance for yourselves and for the aliens who reside among you and have begotten children among you. They shall be to you as citizens of Israel; with you they shall be allotted an inheritance *__among__* the tribes of Israel.]

In Hebrews 11, there is a list in which the Bible tells of a few individuals who were living by faith, and therefore were anticipating a heavenly inheritance based upon that faithfulness.

[Hebrews 11:16: But as it is, they desire a better country, that is, a heavenly one. Therefore God is not ashamed to be called their God; indeed, he has prepared a city for them.]

Who are children of God? When we believe on the Lord Jesus, we are born from above into the family of God, as in Acts 16:31, where the Philippian jailor is told, "Believe [punctiliar; event] on

the Lord Jesus and you ***will be*** [indicative; it will happen] saved."
The children of God are those who have been born from above
into his family.

[Isaiah 28:9-10: Whom will he teach knowledge, and to whom
will he explain the message? Those who are weaned from milk,
those taken from the breast? For it is precept upon precept,
precept upon precept, line upon line, line upon line, here a little,
there a little.]

In this passage in Isaiah, the people to whom he is speaking
(drunken priests and prophets) are scoffing at the way Isaiah is
teaching and warning them, and the way he keeps teaching them.
He was teaching them line upon line, and they did not like that.
"What does he think we are? Babies?" What does the Bible say
about those who use milk?

[Hebrews 5:13-14: for everyone who lives on milk, being still an
infant, is unskilled in the word of righteousness. But solid food
[meat] is for the mature [teleios], for those whose faculties have
been trained by practice to distinguish good from evil.]

Those who use milk ***are*** babies spiritually.

[Isaiah 7:15: [talking about Immanuel] He shall eat curds and
honey by the time he knows how to refuse the evil and choose
the good.]

It takes work to produce curds and honey. Bees produce honey,
but you have to gather it, and it is not an easy process. You might
get stung. But it is worthwhile because there is not much that is
better than mixing butter and honey and putting it on a biscuit.

110

Proverbs tells us how to make curds or butter.

[Proverbs 30:33: For as pressing milk produces curds, and pressing the nose produces blood, so pressing anger produces strife.]

To make butter, you have to press it. Have you ever "pressed" or churned butter? It is hard work. The meat [solid food] is sometimes in the milk, but it takes hard work to get those curds of truth to come together.

Our ability to discern between good and evil will be judged.

[2 Corinthians 5:10: For all of us must appear before the judgment seat of Christ, so that each may receive recompense [be paid for] for what has been done in the body, whether good or evil.]

Recompense is to be paid for your work. This is recompense for works that have been done in the body, whether good or worthless (not even necessarily actively evil). Responsibility and accountability comes with maturity; those who have moved on from the milk.

[Luke 12:48: But the one who did not know and did what deserved a beating will receive a light beating. From everyone to whom much has been given, much will be required; and from the one to whom much has been entrusted, even more will be demanded.]

We are accountable. Those of us in the family are accountable for our actions and our works. The main thing we need to do is grow and move into a level of maturity. We are obviously

111

growing physically, and that is simply natural. But, just as we have to feed the body for it to grow, we also need to feed ourselves spiritually.

[2 Peter 3:18: But grow in the grace and knowledge of our Lord and Savior Jesus Christ. To him be the glory both now and to the day of eternity. Amen.]

Grow in the grace and knowledge of our Lord and Savior Jesus Christ. That is how we mature.

There are several different words in the Bible for children, and they all have to do with different levels of maturity.

All of this leads us to the question, "What is adoption?"

I used to think that using the word "adoption" was simply bad translation. I would ask myself, "How did they get 'adoption' from that word?" There are many good translations out there, and they all are imperfect. However, it was pointed out to me that it might not be a bad translation, but the word itself has changed meaning in English.

Also, there are limitations in English, particularly nuances, which are present in the Greek. Sometimes those nuances are not obvious in the English

We need to change our paradigm. When we read the Bible, we need to put aside the 21st century American mindset and change it to that of Hebrew, Greek, Hebrews writing Greek, and 17th century English. Sometimes, a word that is used in English changes meaning, and later translations use the same words, but we, as a people apply new meanings. There are about 2000 words that have changed meaning since the 17th century, a handful of them drastically, but many modern translations use a lot of the words from the KJV translation. "Adoption" is one of those words.

The etymology of "adoption": 1340, from L. adoptionem (nom. adoptio), noun of action from adoptare "chose for oneself," from ad- "to" + optare "choose, wish" (see "option"). Adopt is a 1548 back-formation.[52]

At that time, the word that was used for placing a child into a family in which he was not born was "affiliation": 1751, "adoption," from Fr. affiliation, from M.L. affiliationem (nom. affiliatio), from L. affiliatus, pp. of affiliare "to adopt a son," from L. ad- "to" + filius "son."[53]

Even today[54], according to Princeton WordNet, the primary meaning of "adoption" in worldwide English is "the act of accepting with approval; favorable reception", with "being placed into a family in which one was not born" being secondary.

When we hear the word "adoption", in 21st century America, the first thing that comes to mind is the image of a child being placed into a family in which he was not born. A child is born into one family, and then, through a legal process, he becomes a member of another family. That is the modern paradigm.

Often, people erroneously teach that when we are saved, we are adopted into the family of God. That contradicts the Bible.

---

[52] *Online Etymology Dictionary,* © *2001 Douglas Harper*
[53] *Online Etymology Dictionary,* © *2001 Douglas Harper*
[54] April 24, 2022.

[John 3:3: Jesus answered him, "Very truly, I tell you, no one can see the kingdom of God without being born from above."]

Acts 16:31 tells us that if we believe [an event], we will be saved; that is when we are born from above. It is a past event from the viewpoint of a member of God's family.

[Romans 8:22-23: We know that the whole creation has been groaning in labor pains until now; and not only the creation, but we ourselves, who have the first fruits of the Spirit, groan inwardly while we **_wait_** for [the[55]] adoption, the redemption of our bodies.]

Romans 8:23 tells us that we wait for the adoption. If we are born from above, we are already in the family. When we accept Jesus as our personal savior [when we believe], we are born from above into the family of God. Being born into the family of God, means that the legal proceedings we call "adoption" are not necessary. I do not need to go down to the courthouse to adopt my children that were born into my family.

[Ephesians 1:5: He destined us for adoption as his children [*huiothesia* – one word] through Jesus Christ, according to the good pleasure of his will.]

In Ephesians 1:5, we find the word "adoption" in context with the word "children". The phrase "adoption as his children" is the translation of the one Greek word, υιοθεσια. This is the same word used in Romans 8:15, and is a compound word that comes from *huios* – son – and *thesis* – to put or to appoint or ordain. There is not any suggestion in this word that it means the legal

---

[55] There is a definite article. This is not just some general waiting, but waiting for a specific event.

114

process of placing a child into a family in which he was not born. This word means "ordain to sonship" or "appoint as a son". A son is a fully mature child.

Ephesians 1:4 tells us that this adoption was chosen for us before the foundation of the world, but when does the appointment take place? Romans 8:19 and 23 answers this question:

[Romans 8:19: For the creation ***waits*** with eager longing for the revealing of the ~~children~~ sons [*huios*] of God;]

[Romans 8:23: and not only the creation, but we ourselves, who have the first fruits of the Spirit, groan inwardly while we wait for [the] adoption, the redemption of our bodies.]

This will take place when our bodies are resurrected, and we wait for that. Jesus Christ was declared the Son of God with Power at his resurrection.

[Romans 1:3-4: ...the gospel concerning his Son, who was descended from David according to the flesh and was declared [designated or defined] ~~to be~~ Son of God with power according to the spirit of holiness ***by resurrection*** from the dead, Jesus Christ our Lord.]

John 3:16 tells us that he was the only one born a son of God. Up until John 3:16, the only ones who were called "sons of God" were Created beings: Angels and Adam. Jesus was born ***the*** Son of God. We can become sons of God.

We are given some insight into what will happen at the resurrection of our bodies.

115

[Philippians 3:21: He will transform the body of our humiliation [humble bodies] that it may be conformed to the body of his glory [his glorious body], by the power that also enables him to make all things subject to himself.]

There is a distinction between "children" and "sons". As mentioned earlier, there are several different words for "child" that are dependent upon levels of maturity.

[Galatians 4:1-2: My point is this: heirs [not outside the family], as long as they are minors [*nepios*], are no better than slaves [servants], though they are the owners of all the property; but they remain under guardians and trustees ***until the date set by the father***.]

Heirs are in the family. As minor children, we are equal to servants and are under guardians until a future date.

A contemporary example of this is at a Jewish young man's bar mitzvah. When he is 13 years old, he becomes a "son of the commandment" and a full member of the synagogue. "*Bar*" means "son" and "*mitzvah*" means "command". The root word, "*tsavah*", means "to enjoin" and is translated as "appoint", "charge", "put", or "command". "*Bar Mitzvah*" and "*Huiothesia*" mean the exact same thing in earthly terms.

Just as in a Jewish family when a boy is placed into the position of a son, in God's family, many of the children of God will be declared sons of God, and will no longer be under guardians and trustees.

What is the distinction and why is it given?

116

As long as we live in this life, we are either being profitable or unprofitable servants.

[Matthew 25:23: His master said to him, 'Well done, good and trustworthy slave; you have been trustworthy in a few things, I will put you in charge of many things; enter into the joy of your master.']

[Luke 17:10: So you also, when you have done all that you were ordered to do, say, 'We are worthless slaves; we have done only what we ought to have done!']

We will be worthless if we have only done that which is our duty to do.[56] Minor children are equal to servants.

What distinguishes children from sons?

[Romans 18:14-15: For all who are led by the Spirit of God are ~~children~~ sons of God. For you did not receive a spirit of slavery to fall back into fear, but you have received a spirit of adoption [*huiothesia*]. When we cry, "Abba! Father!"]

This is the first occurrence of "adoption" or "*huiothesia*".

In verse 14, we see that those who are led by the Spirit of God, **_they_** are the sons of God. It looks like this is something that happens at the exact moment that someone is led by the Spirit. However, this has not happened in this passage. Both the verbs "are led" and "are" ("are" is referring back to those who are led) are present tense verbs. This means that the action is continuous. This is durative action. If you graph the action of the present

---

[56] But we better do our duty, or else!

tense, you use a straight line. The present tense is "I am running". Action can stop, and it is no longer continuous.

"For all who *__are being led__* by the Spirit of God…" is both durative and passive. The action is happening to them. "I am leading" is present, active and "I am being led" is present, passive.

Because the present tense expresses durative action, the action of "being led by the Spirit of God" can continue for a while, and then stop. The other verb, "are", which is referring back to those who are being led by the Spirit of God, is also in the present tense, and can be expressed as "they are being sons". As long as we are "being led" by the Spirit of God, we are "being" the sons of God. As soon as we stop "being led" by the Spirit of God, we are no longer "being" or "behaving" ourselves as sons of God.

For some examples, there are similar uses of the present tense elsewhere in Romans.

[Romans 8:5: For those who live [present, active; are being; in accord; "live" is not in the verse] according to the flesh set their minds [present, active; they are minding] on the things of the flesh, but those who live according to the Spirit set their minds on the things of the Spirit [or spirit].]

These are being in accord with flesh or being in accord with spirit.

[Romans 8:6-7: To set the mind on the flesh is death, but to set the mind on the spirit is life and peace. For this reason the mind that is set on the flesh is hostile to God; it does not submit to God's law—indeed it cannot.]

118

If we are in accord with flesh and not with spirit, we are not subject to the law of God, and then we are not subject to the Spirit of God. We are lawless.

[Romans 8:8: and those who are [present, active, participle; those who are being] in the flesh [minding the things of the flesh in verse 5] cannot [*"ou"* emphatic "not"] ***please God***.]

To be led by the Spirit of God is to be spiritually minded and to behave ourselves as sons of God and to live in such a way as to please Him.

If Romans 8:14 is saying that we are ***now*** sons of God, then the sons of God have been revealed and we are in our glorified bodies. I certainly do not feel very glorified. We are obviously not presently in our glorified bodies.

[Galatians 4:6-7: And because you are ~~children~~ sons, God has sent the Spirit of his Son into our hearts, crying, "Abba! Father!" So you are no longer a slave but a ~~child~~ son, and if a ~~child~~ son then also an heir of God, through Christ.]

This is not saying that we are literally sons of God at this moment, just as we cannot say we are no longer servants of God. We are still in this body of death, but we are to live like a son; we are in the position of a son to show ourselves mindful of mature things. To live like a son, we must use Jesus as our example.

[1 Peter 2:21-23: For to this you have been called, because Christ also ***suffered*** for you, leaving you an ***example***, so that you should follow in his steps. "He committed no sin, and no deceit was found in his mouth." When he was abused, he did not return

119

abuse; when he suffered, he did not threaten; but he entrusted himself to the one who judges justly.]

Who did he entrust himself to? Who is the one who judges righteously? In Luke 23:46, he said, "Father, into your hands I commend my spirit", and 1 Peter 1:17 tells us that the Father "judges all people impartially according to their deeds". We are to entrust ourselves to things of God if we are to live as sons.

We are given some examples by which we should live.

[Philippians 2:5-8: Let the same mind be in you that was in Christ Jesus, who, though he was in the form of God, did not regard equality with God as something to be exploited, but emptied himself, taking the form of a slave, being born in human likeness. And being found in human form, he **_humbled himself_** and became **_obedient_** to the point of death – even death on a cross.]

What does it mean when it says, "he was in the form of God"? "Was in" is a present, active, participle, and it is not simply "being", but it is a stronger meaning that implies something which was a particular way from the beginning. Not necessarily the ultimate beginning, but from the beginning of the reference.

A good example to see this clearly is found in James.

[James 2:15-17: If a brother or sister is naked and lacks daily food, and one of you says to them, "Go in peace; keep warm and eat your fill," and yet you do not supply their bodily needs, what is the good of that? So faith by itself, if it has no works, is dead.]

"Is", used here with "naked and lacks daily food" is not the usual verb for "is" (*einai*), but this word (*huparchO*), originally means

The Warnings In Hebrews, Adoption, and Why We Are All Going to Hell

"to make a beginning". It means "to begin" or "come into being". Although it is used almost synonymously with "*einai*" to mean "a thing existing right now", it also looks backward to a previous condition which continues on into the present. In this verse, we could paraphrase it as, "If a brother or sister, having been in this destitute condition, is found by you in that condition…" "*Einai*" would simply state the present fact of destitution. This is not easily translated directly.[57]

"He **_was_** in the form of God." It is this way now, but also looks backward to the beginning. The word does not inherently imply "eternal" but only implies prior existence before the time of which is being spoken. In this case it is speaking of the pre-incarnate being of Christ, and Christ **_is_** eternal, but that is not the reference for this passage.

"He was in the **_form_** of God." What is the "form" of God? From the paradigm of which this is written it does not mean "shape". It is from the word "*morphe*", from which we get the English suffix "-morph", which means "form" or "structure", to which we add a prefix so that it means a form or structure of a specified kind, such as "endomorph". We also get the word "morph", which means "to be transformed". We can "morph" a photo from one image to another. Both of those words seem to be shortened from "*metamorph*". "Metamorphosis", which means "a profound change from one form to another", as in a caterpillar into a butterfly. ("Meta" denotes "change", so metamorphosis means to literally change form.) It is used in the **_complete_** sense of the word to create the idea of that which has in itself the nature and characteristics of the one to whom it is referring. Therefore, it is permanently identified with that nature and character. This is not

---

[57] The CLV states it well: "If a brother or sister should be belonging to the naked…"

121

the same idea as "*schema*" or "fashion", which appeals to the senses and can change. "*Morphe*" or "form" is identified with the essence of what is being discussed, whereas "*schema*" or "fashion" is the outwardly appearance, and you can see words in English that have derived from these Greek words.

[Matthew 17:2: And he was transfigured before them, and his face shone like the sun, and his clothes became dazzling white.]

Here, the word "*metamorphO*" is used; it is the word "transfigured". "*Meta*" is "change" and "*morphe*" is "form". It was not just an outward appearance that changed, although the outward form is what was observable.

[Mark 16:12-13: After this he appeared in another form to two of them, as they were walking into the country. And they went back and told the rest, but they did not believe them.]

He appeared to them in another "form". Essence.

[1 Corinthians 7:31: and those who deal with the world as though they had no dealings with it. For the present form [fashion] of this world is passing away.]

Here, "*schema*" is used. This is something that is superficial. The fashion will change, but the essence will remain.

We can see the distinctions between these two words. He was in the ***form*** of God. As applied here to the way in which the essence of God presents itself. In English, there is not really a single word that conveys this meaning. However, using what we learned from the "trivial" education,[58] we can see that "form", contrary to the

---

[58] See the study on the Trivium and Quadrivium.

idea of "shape" which we try to give it, can try to conceive of the very essence of Godhood or deity itself. It is not identical with it. It is not the exact same thing which we cannot look upon, however, it *is* identified with it as an appropriate expression of a perfect essence. It is not just an outward appearance, but it is something that comes from within that perfect being, and it is something into which that perfect being unfolds to make a complete picture.

To say that he was in the ***form*** of God is to say that he is one with God in unity, but not one in uniqueness. This expression of deity in a man has its roots in the expression of deity in the eternity of God's being. This verse is marking the being of Christ in the eternity before creation. The form of God is identified with the being of God, so Christ being in the form of God is here identified with the being, nature, personality, and deity of God.

This form is not identical, but it is dependent. This implies that it can be laid aside temporarily, which is what he did while on this earth. He was both fully God and fully man, but lived as a man.

"Did not regard equality with God as something to be ***exploited***." The word "exploited" has been translated in various translations as "robbery" (thought it not robbery), "something to be held onto", "grasped", "pillaging", "usurpation", "a treasure to be tightly grasped", "a thing to be seized", "something to be used for his own advantage", and I got tired of looking after that. The word can mean "a violent seizure of property", but it can also mean "something one can claim title to by gripping or grasping", whether gaining it or simply holding onto it. (It also has some other shades of meanings, none of which are applicable here.) Here, in this verse, it is used in the latter sense.

If it were the former sense, that of gaining it through seizure, then in conjunction with the statement that he was in the form of God, he did not think it was robbery to be equal with God, then when joined with the following phrase, "he emptied himself" would logically lead to the contradictory conclusion, "he claimed and asserted equality with God, held fast to it, and relinquished it."

Instead, if you take the word as the second meaning of a "highly prized possession", it is easy to understand that Paul is saying that Christ, being in the form of God before his earthly incarnation, did not see his divine equality as something to hold onto at all costs, although it is something that is highly prized. To the contrary, he laid aside this form and took the nature of man upon himself.

It says he emptied himself and took the ***form*** of a slave. He took the essence, not just the outward appearance, and he came to be in the likeness of man.

The emphasis in this passage is upon his humiliation. His equality with God is stated to bring emphasis upon his human incarnation as a contrast. His purpose was to identify with humanity, not draw attention to his divinity. If he had come into the world as deity, the world would have been astounded. There would have been parades and speeches, but would the world have been saved? We are to walk by faith, not by sight. He laid aside one prized possession, his divinity, temporarily for the prize of humanity, and to do this, he himself became a man.

How did he do this? "He emptied himself." He laid aside the "form" of God. This does not mean that he laid aside his divine nature, just the state of divinity, which he exchanged for the form of a servant. He was still the same person. He did not lay aside his *self*, neither was he changed into a *mere* man. His *self* was still deity. It is not that he was unable to assert equality with God; he was able ***not to assert it***.

"Taking the form of a slave [servant]". The same sense here is the same as with "form of God". This is not the physical shape, but the essence of the servant's being. This is in contrast to being equal with God in the previous verse. He was here to set an example for us, and as such, he set aside his sovereignty and focused on service.

"Being born in human likeness." "Becoming"; not "was", but "became". It is not that he was simply a human, but that he entered into a new state from an old state. This is "likeness", not "form". "Form" implies essence; it is reality. He was in the form of God; he took the form of a servant. He really is God, and he really was a servant of men. But, "likeness" shows that he outwardly resembled what men are. He was like men with a real likeness, but this likeness did not express his whole self. He could not appear to men as God. In Exodus 33, Moses had asked to see God's glory, but what was God's response?

[Exodus 33:20: But," he said, "you cannot see my face; for no one shall see me and live."]

To be seen by men and appeal to men, he could only appear as a man, and only as a real and complete man.

[Isaiah 53:2b: ...he had no form or majesty that we should look at him, nothing in his appearance that we should desire him.]

His essence (his deity) could not be a part of his human existence. He was like men, but not identical. Likeness is similarity, but not identical sameness. His humanity was as real as his deity. He was both fully God and fully man.

"And being found in human form." Here is the word "*schema*" again. It is "fashion"; external and not essence, as in the form of God. Different translations put "appearance", "fashion", "condition", and "a man in his external form". There is a contrast between what he appeared to be to men and what he was in *self*. But, this external form was *__real__*.

"He humbled himself." He voluntarily humiliated himself. This is not the same as emptying himself as in verse 7; this is the manifestation of that self-emptying. This is the example that Paul is impressing upon the Philippians. This God-man made the ultimate sacrifice, emptied himself, and humbled himself, and they were to do the same thing, although they did not have as much to sacrifice. They were to use him as their example.

"He humbled himself and became obedient." Obedience is "giving ear to"; it has more to do with faithfulness than simply with successfully following a list of rules.

[Acts 7:39: Our ancestors were unwilling to obey him; instead, they pushed him aside, and in their hearts they turned back to Egypt]

They did what they were supposed to do, but they were not faithful. I know that we can only judge actions, so we tend to use the word "obey" in the sense of doing what you are told, but in the Bible, this word implies putting your heart to it (faithfulness) more than simply successfully doing what you are told.

"Became obedient to the point of death – even death on a cross."
The ultimate humiliation. He not only submitted to death, but it
was the death of a criminal. Those who were hung on a cross
were reviled. After crucifixion their bodies were thrown outside
the city into the trash. Out of all the interred bodies that have been
discovered in archaeological digs in Jerusalem, there has only
been one ever found that had been crucified. (Of course, that
means there were two; Jesus was entombed, but *__he__* is still using
his body.)

Death by crucifixion was so low that there is a curse against it.

[Deuteronomy 21.23a: his corpse must not remain all night upon
the tree; you shall bury him that same day, for anyone hung on a
tree is under God's curse.]

Even the Gentiles used crucifixion only for slaves and criminals.

__This__ is why there is shame associated with the cross.

[Hebrews 12:2: looking to Jesus the pioneer and perfecter of our
faith, who for the sake of [instead of] the joy that was set before
him endured the cross, disregarding its shame, and has taken his
seat at the right hand of the throne of God.]

The death on the cross was a stumbling block to the Jews because
of the curse, and to the Gentiles, it was pure foolishness.

[1 Corinthians 1:23: but we proclaim Christ crucified, a
stumbling block to Jews and foolishness to Gentiles]

To the Jews it was a curse straight from God. The Gentiles
dressed up their gods with all sorts of niceties, such as being

attractive and dressing nicely. So, to both groups, worshipping a criminal who had been crucified was not simply odd, it was just **_wrong_**. But, what does the Bible say?

[Galatians 3:13a: but we proclaim Christ crucified, a stumbling block to Jews and foolishness to Gentiles]

Interestingly, in the Talmud, the Messiah's image had been obscured from what the Scriptures said and made it so he would resemble what the Gentile world pictured. He would have been unrecognizable to anyone who was not familiar with the Scriptures themselves. Just as the Jews wanted a king like the Gentile nations had, they created a savior in the same likeness as the Gentile nations had created.

[Philippians 2:5-8: Let the same mind be in you that was in Christ Jesus, who, though he was in the form of God, did not regard equality with God as something to be exploited, but emptied himself, taking the form of a slave, being born in human likeness. And being found in human form, he humbled himself and became **_obedient_** to the point of death— even death on a cross.]

[Hebrews 5:8: Although he was a Son, he learned obedience through what he suffered.]

He was a **_son_**, yet he still was not exempted from being obedient. He did not have to learn how to obey; he had to be obedient through the infirmities of a severe human experience.

[John 8:29: And the one who sent me is with me; he has not left me alone, for I always do what is pleasing to him.]

Obedience is a disciplining process. Not a discipline out of an inclination to disobedience, but a disciplining through which he was perfected as our high priest. He always did his Father's will, but he grew in experience as well as in wisdom and stature and in the power of commiseration with us.

[John 4:34: Jesus said to them, "My food is to do the will of him who sent me and to complete his work."]

The emphasis is on the end, more than the process. This is not a list of thou shalls and thou shall nots; this has an eye on the prize for completing the work.

[Mark 14:36: He said, "Abba, Father, for you all things are possible; remove this cup from me; yet, not what I want, but what you want."]

[Matthew 10:24: "A disciple is not above the teacher, nor a slave above the master;"]

[Romans 8:15: For you did not receive a spirit of slavery to fall back into fear, but you have received a spirit of adoption. When we cry, "Abba! Father!"]

We also can cry "Abba! Father!"

[Galatians 4:6: And because you are children sons, God has sent the Spirit of his Son into our hearts, crying, "Abba! Father!"]

[Hebrews 12:2: looking to Jesus the pioneer [leader] and perfecter of our faith, who for the sake of [instead of] the joy that was set before him endured the cross, disregarding its shame, and has taken his seat at the right hand of the throne of God.]

Faith is a noun; it is a lifestyle. Our faith is our ability to please him. Because Jesus was a good and faithful servant, he endured the cross, which is more than simply enduring crucifixion. He despised the shame of the cross, but was nonetheless obedient. He was not only obedient in actions, but he despised disobedience, as well. Shame comes from disobedience, and being set down at the right hand of God, is what it means to be an overcomer.

[2 Timothy 1:7: for God did not give us a spirit of cowardice [timidity], but rather a spirit of power and of love and of self-discipline.]

He has given us a spirit of power [*dunamis*; dynamo]; he has given us a spirit of love [*agape*]; he has given us a spirit of self-discipline [sanity; control; both in ourselves and to project it into others]. We have power, agape love, and a sound mind.

Who are the sons of God today?

[Genesis 6:4: The Nephilim were on the earth in those days—and also afterward—when the sons of God went in to the daughters of humans [Adam], who bore children to them. These were the heroes that were of old, warriors of renown.]

[Job 1:6: One day the heavenly beings [sons of God] came to present themselves before the LORD, and Satan also came among them.]

[Job 38:7: when the morning stars sang together and all the heavenly beings [sons of God] shouted for joy?]

[Luke 3:38: son of Enos, son of Seth, son of Adam, son of God.]

Only created beings (angels and Adam) and Jesus are referred to in the Bible as sons of God today. Just as there is order and rank among the sons of God today, there will also one day be order and rank among the other sons of God.

[Daniel 10:13: But the prince of the kingdom of Persia opposed me twenty-one days. So Michael, one of the chief princes, came to help me, and I left him there with the prince of the kingdom of Persia.]

[Ephesians 6:12: For our struggle is not against enemies of blood and flesh, but against the rulers, against the authorities, against the cosmic powers of this present darkness, against the spiritual forces of evil in the heavenly places.]

These passages show the angels, whether fallen or not, are known as the sons of God, and they are the rulers and authorities and cosmic powers in the heavens today. And not only are they the rulers today, we are told that Satan is the god of this world.

[Ephesians 2:2: in which you once lived, following the course of this world, following the ruler of the power of the air, the spirit that is now at work among those who are disobedient.]

Satan is *the* ruler of the demons and other evil beings. Jesus even calls Satan "the ruler of this world" in John 16:11; literally, *the* chief of this world.

[John 16:11: ...about judgment, because the ruler of this world has been condemned.]

When studying sons and adoption, we know what a son is, and we know when the placing of sons will take place, but who is it that will be the sons of God in the age to come?

[Revelation 12:9: The great dragon was thrown down, that ancient serpent, who is called the Devil and Satan, the deceiver of the whole world—he was thrown down to the earth, and his angels were thrown down with him.]

This is taking place around the middle of the tribulation period, and the powers in the heavenly places will be kicked out! Those who have been appointed to sonship will then begin to rule from the heavens, when it is time.

[Revelation 2:26-28: To everyone who conquers and continues to do my works to the end, I will give authority over the nations; to rule [shepherd] them with an iron rod, as when clay pots are shattered – even as I also received authority from my Father. To the one who conquers I will also give the morning star.]

What is the "morning star"?

[Revelation 22:16: "It is I, Jesus, who sent my angel to you with this testimony for the churches. I am the root and the descendant of David, the bright morning star."]

He will give the authority himself. The Kingdom of the Heavens is Christ's Kingdom. This falls in line with the promise of power over the nations that was given in Revelation 2:26.

The star was an ancient emblem of sovereignty in almost every culture, but especially throughout the Bible, which uses them to represent both sovereignty and divine leadership.

[Numbers 24:17: I see him, but not now; I behold him, but not near — a star shall come out of Jacob, and a scepter shall rise out of Israel;]

[Matthew 2:2a: "Where is the child who has been born king of the Jews? For we observed his star…"]

A king comes to judge and punish, but also to cheer and brighten. A good king brings joy to his people, just as he brings discipline. A free people cannot be a lawless people.

[2 Peter 1:19: So we have the prophetic message more fully confirmed. You will do well to be attentive to this as to a lamp shining in a dark place, until the day dawns and the morning star rises in your hearts.]

God gives us prophecy in order that we will know what is coming. If you and I were in a dark cave and I had a lamp, you could see the light from far off. But, the closer you got to the light, the more clearly you would be able to see. The more clearly you can see, the safer you are from pitfalls. We are told not to set dates, but we are also given signs to know that the time is fast approaching. An example of that we can look to what is going on in the Middle East right now in relation to the prophecy in Ezekiel 38 and 39. For the first time in history, since that prophecy was written, it can now come to pass. Israel has something that Russia (or the people who have ever lived in the land we now call "Russia") wants, Russia is allied with Iran, Iraq is out of the picture, and Egypt, although always at war with Israel before, is now abiding by a treaty signed about few decades back. Never before have all these circumstances been present at the same time, so we know that it is now possible for it to happen.

When the Messiah comes to make war, he does not come alone.

[Revelation 17:14: [This is talking about the ten horns; they are united under the Beast] they will make war on the Lamb, and the Lamb will conquer them, for he is Lord of lords and King of kings, and those with him are **_called_** and **_chosen_** and **_faithful_**."]

"Called", "chosen", and "faithful" are adjectives describing the lords and kings that are with him.

What did he promise the apostles for faithfulness?

[Matthew 19:27-28: Then Peter said in reply, "Look, we have left everything and followed you. What then will we have?" Jesus said to them, "Truly I tell you, at the renewal of all things, when the Son of Man is seated on the throne of his glory, you who have followed me will also sit on twelve thrones, judging the twelve tribes of Israel.]

When will this promise be fulfilled? When the Son of Man is seated on the throne of his glory. What will happen? Those who have followed him will sit upon twelve thrones. What will they be doing? Judging the twelve tribes of Israel. This takes place during the Millennial reign of Christ over the Earth.

This things are challenging; these things are not easy.

[Revelation 21:7: Those who conquer [he who overcomes; singular; it is an individual proposition] will inherit these things, and I will be their [his; singular] God and they [he; singular] will be my ~~children~~ sons [son].]

The one who overcomes will inherit. Who is it that inherits? Sons. Overcomers will be sons.

[Hebrews 11:16: But as it is, they desire a better country, that is, a heavenly one. Therefore God is not ashamed to be called their God; indeed, he has prepared a city for them.]

[1 Corinthians 15:57-58: But thanks be to God, who gives us the *victory* through our Lord Jesus Christ. Therefore, my beloved [brethren; Matthew 12:50 says brethren do the will of the father], be *steadfast*, *immovable*, always *excelling in the work* of the Lord, because you know that in the Lord your labor is not in vain.]

He who overcomes will inherit. Sons will inherit. Overcomers are those who desire something better than the status quo and they persevere until the end. The faithful are brethren. Sons will be victors and will receive a victor's crown, and they will be ruling and reigning in the coming Kingdom of our Lord.

Do you want to simply be a child or do you want to be adopted as a son?

Why We Are All Going To Hell

There are four different words that have been translated as "hell" in various translations. None of them are the lake of fire forever and ever. Using hell as the lake of fire forever and ever is putting a man-made doctrine onto the word "hell", and that doctrine comes mainly from errant Roman Catholic teachings. Although its origin is with Roman Catholicism, the idea is really popular with fire-and-brimstone preachers to instill fear into people to whom they are preaching, and while there is much to fear, that preaching is misdirected.

The word "hell" is found 54 times in the KJV, 15 times in the NRSV (two of those are in the Apocrypha in 2 Esdras 2:29 and 7:36), 15 times in the NASB (all in the NT), 15 in the Amplified, 14 in the NIV, 20 in the NLT, 13 in the ASV (all NT), 14 in the ESV (all NT), 15 in the NET (all NT), and it is not found at all in Rotherham's (one of the best translations; I know some Greek teachers who require their students to use this translation for class), the CLV, Weymouth's, or Young's. (These last four are literal translations; the underlying words are transliterated, and thereby avoid this controversy.)

"Hades" and "Sheol", two of the words that are sometimes translated as "hell", are simply the unseen world of the dead.[59] Hades is Greek and Sheol is Hebrew. Both the wicked and the righteous go there.

"Tartarus" is, in Greek tradition, the lowest pit of Hades, and in the Bible is used only in relation to angels who are being

---

[59] Technically, "Hades" is the name of the Greek god of the underworld, but it has become the name of the unseen world of the dead by association.

punished. It is found only in 2 Peter 2:4 and in the book of Enoch, which is an "approved" extra-Biblical book that is quoted in the canon of Scripture. Tartarus is not the final destination for the angels who are held in bondage there; they have a future judgment coming.

"Gehenna" is the word which should be of primary interest to most believers. If Gehenna is the lake of fire forever and ever, there are some serious doctrinal and theological contradictions in the Bible. Gehenna is never used as the lake of fire forever and ever, however, it is always used as a warning to those who are in the family, not those who are outside the family. If Gehenna is the lake of fire forever and ever, there is nothing in which we can ever be secure, and there is contradiction with the passages that teach the familial security of the believer. Once you are in the family, you are in the family, but the threat of hell (Gehenna) is a real danger to the believer.

The Four Words for Hell & Where They Are Found:

Hades: Matthew 11:23, 16:18, Luke 10:15, 16:23, Acts 2:27, 31, Revelation 1:18, 6:8, 20:13-14.

Tartarus: 2 Peter 2:4, Enoch 20:2.[60]

Gehenna: Matthew 5:22;29;30, 10:28, 18:9, 23:15;33, Mark 9:43;45;47, Luke 12:5, James 3:6.

---

[60] This reference is included because it shows how Jewish Christians would have understood what is being taught.

Hades verses:

[Matthew 11:23-24: And you, Capernaum, will you be exalted to heaven? No, you will be brought down to Hades. For if the deeds of power done in you had been done in Sodom, it would have remained until this day. But I tell you that on the day of judgment it will be more tolerable for the land of Sodom than for you."]

[Matthew 16:18: And I tell you, you are Peter, and on this rock I will build my church, and the gates of Hades will not prevail against it.]

[Luke 10:15: And you, Capernaum, will you be exalted to heaven? No, you will be brought down to Hades.]

[Luke 16:22-23: The poor man died and was carried away by the angels to be with Abraham [be Abraham's bosom]. The rich man also died and was buried. In Hades, where he was being tormented, he looked up and saw Abraham far away with Lazarus by his side [in his bosom].]

[Acts 2:27, 30-31: For you will not abandon my soul to Hades, or let your Holy One experience corruption... Since he was a prophet, he knew that God had sworn with an oath to him that he would put one of his descendants on his throne. Foreseeing this, David spoke of the resurrection of the Messiah, saying, 'He was not abandoned to Hades, nor did his flesh experience corruption.']

[Revelation 1:17-18: When I saw him, I fell at his feet as though dead. But he placed his right hand on me, saying, "Do not be afraid; I am the first and the last, and the living one. I was dead, and see, I am alive forever and ever; and I have the keys of Death and of Hades.]

[Revelation 6:8a: I looked and there was a pale green horse! Its rider's name was Death, and Hades followed with him.]

[Revelation 20:13-14a: And the sea gave up the dead that were in it, Death and Hades gave up the dead that were in them, and all were judged according to what they had done. Then Death and Hades were thrown into the lake of fire.]

Tartarus verses:[61]

[2 Peter 2:4: For if God did not spare the angels when they sinned, but cast them into hell [Tartarus] and committed them to chains [pits] of deepest darkness to be kept until the judgment...]

[Enoch 20:1-2: And these are the names of the holy angels who watch. Uriel, one of the holy angels, who is over the world and over Tartarus. [And then it goes on to name some other angels and describes what they preside over.]]

Gehenna verses:

[Matthew 5:22;29-30: But I say to you that if you are angry with a brother or sister, you will be liable to judgment; and if you insult[62] a brother or sister, you will be liable to the council; and

---

[61] This word is also found in the LXX in the book of Job in 40:20 and 41:32 where Satan is a captive in Tartarus, but it is left untranslated in the English translations that I have seen, and since it is untranslated I did not include those verses. However, it is worth studying.

[62] "Say *raca* to"; an obscure but serious expression of verbal abuse. Equivalent to contempt for his head.

if you say, 'You fool,'[63] you will be liable to the hell of fire... If your right eye causes you to sin, tear it out and throw it away; it is better for you to lose one of your members than for your whole body to be thrown into hell. And if your right hand causes you to sin, cut it off and throw it away; it is better for you to lose one of your members than for your whole body to go into hell.]

[Matthew 10:28: Do not fear those who kill the body but cannot kill the soul; rather fear him who can destroy both soul and body in hell.]

[Matthew 18:9: And if your eye causes you to stumble, tear it out and throw it away; it is better for you to enter life with one eye than to have two eyes and to be thrown into the hell of fire.]

[Matthew 23:15, 33: Woe to you, scribes and Pharisees, hypocrites! For you cross sea and land to make a single convert, and you make the new convert twice as much a child of hell as yourselves... You snakes, you brood of vipers! How can you escape being sentenced to hell?]

[Mark 9:43, 45, 47: If your hand causes you to stumble, cut it off; it is better for you to enter life maimed than to have two hands and to go to hell, to the unquenchable fire. And if your foot causes you to stumble, cut it off; it is better for you to enter life lame than to have two feet and to be thrown into hell. And if your eye causes you to stumble, tear it out; it is better for you to enter the kingdom of God with one eye than to have two eyes and to be thrown into hell.]

---

[63] This is the Greek word *morE*, which expresses contempt for a man's heart, as opposed to his head.

[Luke 12:4-5: "I tell you, my friends, do not fear those who kill the body, and after that can do nothing more. But I will warn you whom to fear: fear him who, after he has killed, has authority to cast into hell. Yes, I tell you, fear him!]

[James 3:5b-6: How great a forest is set ablaze by a small fire! And the tongue is a fire. The tongue is placed among our members as a world of iniquity; it stains the whole body, sets on fire the cycle of nature, and is itself set on fire by hell.]

[2 Esdras 2:29: My power will protect you [literally, My hands will cover you], so that your children may not see hell.]

[2 Esdras 7:36: The pit [place] of torment shall appear, and opposite it shall be the place of rest; and the furnace of hell shall be disclosed, and opposite it the paradise of delight.]

> The English word "hell" comes from the Old English hel, helle, "nether world, abode of the dead, infernal regions," from Proto-Germanic haljo "the underworld" (cognates: f. Old Frisian helle, Dutch hel, Old Norse hel, German Hölle, Gothic halja) "the underworld," literally "concealed place" (compare Old Norse hellir "cave, cavern"), from Proto Indo-European kel- to cover, conceal.
>
> The English word may be in part from Old Norse Hel (from Proto-Germanic halija "one who covers up or hides something"), in Norse mythology the name of Loki's daughter,[64] who rules over the evil

---

[64] Her name is "Hel" and the expression "go to Hel" literally means I want you to die.

dead in *Niflheim*, the lowest of all worlds (*nifl* "mist"). Transfer of a pagan concept and word to a Christian idiom. In Middle English, also of the *Limbus Patrum*, place where the Patriarchs, Prophets, etc. awaited the Atonement. Used in the KJV for Old Testament Hebrew Sheol and New Testament Greek Hades and Gehenna. Used figuratively for "state of misery, any bad experience" since at least late 14c. As an expression of disgust, etc., first recorded 1670s.[65]

As you can see, if "hell" is the lake of fire forever and ever, then we are all in trouble because we are all going to hell. What we need to look at is what the underlying words mean in the text, which will therefore let us see what the text means.

To begin with, we are not angels, so Tartarus is only of interest to us if we are studying angels.[66]

Hades or Sheol is something every single one of us will have to deal with, unless, of course, the Lord returns before we die.

[Psalm 16:8-11: I keep the LORD always before me; because he is at my right hand, I shall not be moved. Therefore my heart is glad, and my soul rejoices; my body also rests secure. For you do not give me up to Sheol, or let your faithful one see the Pit. You show me the path of life. In your presence there is fullness of joy; in your right hand are pleasures forevermore.]

---

[65] Online Etymology Dictionary, © 2001-2014 Douglas Harper.
[66] Which really is a fascinating study, especially the way all this relates to fallen angels and Nephilim, but is beyond the scope of this study on hell.

[Acts 2:29-32: "Fellow Israelites [brethren], I may say to you confidently of our ancestor David that he both died and was buried, and his tomb is with us to this day. Since he was a prophet, he knew that God had sworn with an oath to him that he would put one of his descendants on his throne. Foreseeing this, David spoke of the resurrection of the Messiah, saying, "He was not abandoned to Hades, nor did his flesh experience corruption." This Jesus God raised up, and of that all of us are witnesses.]

Here is both an OT and a NT example that uses Sheol and Hades. Many translations translate these as "hell". That is not necessarily a bad translation, but the way we tend to use the word today, translating it as hell leads to confusion.

When Jesus Christ went to hell after dying on the cross, he did not go to the lake of fire forever and ever.[67] In fact, he told the thief on the cross, "Truly I tell you, today you will be with me in Paradise."[68] Paradise, in Jewish theology is the part of the unseen world of the dead where those who are righteous are held until resurrection. In the LXX, it is used as a reference to the Garden of Eden. It is also called Abraham's Bosom. Paradise is always used for the blessed.

The death of the Lord Jesus Christ on the cross was sufficient to save every person.[69]

In Acts 16:31 the Philippian jailor is told to believe (event) and he will be saved. Once we believe, we have heavenly DNA. We

---

[67] His soul went to Hades. His spirit went to be with the Father and his body was in the tomb. See also Luke 23:46 and Matthew 27:60.

[68] There is some debate about the correct placement of the comma. It may be, "Today I tell you, you will be with me in Paradise."

[69] 2 Corinthians 5:15.

are in the family, and that can never change. However, there are consequences for misbehaving.[70] Anyone who believes on the Lord Jesus will be saved, but we are all still subject to Hades/Sheol.

This brings us to Gehenna.

We will begin by looking at several passages that are talking about the lake of fire and see if Gehenna and the lake of fire forever and ever are the same thing.

[Revelation 19:20: And the beast was captured, and with it the false prophet who had performed in its presence the signs by which he deceived those who had received the mark of the beast and those who worshiped its image. These two were thrown alive into the lake of fire that burns with sulfur.]

[Revelation 20:10: And the devil who had deceived them was thrown into the lake of fire and sulfur, where the beast and the false prophet were, and they will be tormented day and night forever and ever.]

[Revelation 20:14: Then Death and Hades were thrown into the lake of fire. This is the second death, the lake of fire.]

[Revelation 20:12, 15: And I saw the dead, great and small, standing before the throne, and books were opened. Also another book was opened, the book of life. And the dead were judged according to their works, as recorded in the books... and anyone

---

[70] Do not make the mistake of always associating judgments in reference to someone else. Most of the judgments in the NT are not made against those outside the family, but against believers.

whose name was not found written in the book of life was thrown into the lake of fire.]

Here we see the beast, the false prophet, the devil, death, hades, and those who are not found written in the book of life; they are all thrown into the lake of fire. Those who are not in the family are tossed in.

[Revelation 21:8: But as for the cowardly, the faithless, the polluted, the murderers, the fornicators, the sorcerers, the idolaters, and all liars, their ~~place~~ part will be in the lake that burns with fire and sulfur, which is the second death."]

This word that is translated as "place" in the NRSV is the word "*meros*"; it means "part" or "share", as contrasted to the whole.[71]

[Luke 15:11-12: Then Jesus said, "There was a man who had two sons. The younger of them said to his father, 'Father, give me the ***share*** of the property that will belong to me.' So he divided his property between them.]

This word "share" is the same word that is used in Revelation 21:8.

His share will be consumed. He can lose (or use up) his inheritance. A person in the family can lose reward or privileges or the right to rule and reign with the Lord in his coming

---

[71] The NRSV is a very good translation overall, but sometimes they do things that are baffling. Almost every translation has either "part", "portion", or "share", but for some reason they chose to use "place".

Kingdom. He can lose his position *__within__* the family, but cannot lose his place *__in__* the family.[72]

[1 Corinthians 3:13-15: the work of each builder will become visible, for the Day will disclose it, because it will be revealed with fire, and the fire will test what sort of work each has done. If what has been built on the foundation survives, the builder will receive a reward. If the work is burned up, the builder will suffer loss; the builder will be saved, but only as through fire.]

"Their ~~place~~ [part] will be in the lake that burns with fire and sulfur."

[John 13:3-7a: Jesus, knowing that the Father had given all things into his hands, and that he had come from God and was going to God, got up from the table, took off his outer robe, and tied a towel around himself. Then he poured water into a basin and began to wash the disciples' feet and to wipe them with the towel that was tied around him. He came to Simon Peter, who said to him, "Lord, are you going to wash my feet?" Jesus answered, "You do not know now what I am doing…"]

"You do not know now what I am doing." I feel fairly certain that Peter knew that Jesus was washing his feet, so there has to be a lesson that is deeper than the simple physical lesson that is being taught.

[John 13:7b-8: "…later you will understand." Peter said to him, "You will never wash my feet." Jesus answered, "Unless I wash you, you have no **share** with me."]

---

[72] This idea is demonstrated in Numbers 18:20 as well in which Moses is told he will neither have an inheritance or a part because of his disobedience. The LXX uses the same word we are discussing for "part" or "share".

The word "share" in this passage is also the same word that we saw in Revelation 21:8.

Jesus washed Peter's feet. He helped him have a clean walk. Without that clean walk, he would have no share with Jesus. Unless our walk is clean, _we_ will have no share with Jesus.

[Luke 10:38-42: Now as they went on their way, he entered a certain village, where a woman named Martha welcomed him into her home. She had a sister named Mary, who sat at the Lord's feet and listened to what he was saying.[73] But Martha was distracted by her many tasks; so she came to him and asked, "Lord, do you not care that my sister has left me to do all the work by myself? Tell her then to help me."[74] But the Lord answered her, "Martha, Martha, you are worried and distracted by many things;[75] there is need of only one thing. Mary has chosen the better _**part**_, which will not be taken away from her."]

The better part or better share is sitting at the feet of Jesus and listening to what he has to say. _**That**_ is the part that is of such great value. "There is need of only one thing." That is why we study theology; that is why we study the Word of God as well as the words of God.

We may fail to be overcomers. We may be hurt of the second death. The testing in the lake of fire will cause us to lose our part or our share, although we ourselves will be saved as though

---

[73] You are going to see a contrast here.

[74] He did not tell Mary to help.

[75] What is for lunch? Do I need to add more mutton to the stew? Do the potatoes need more chives?

through fire. No matter what we may lose, we will still be saved spiritually; we will still be in the family.

There is something that we can do to help ensure that we will have a share with the Lord. He may cleanse us so that we can have a clean walk, but we *have to walk that walk*.

[2 Corinthians 5:9-11a: So whether we[76] are at home or away, we make it our aim [talking about works] to please him. For all of us must appear before the judgment seat of Christ, so that each may *receive recompense for* what *has been done* in the body, *whether good or evil*. Therefore, knowing the fear of the Lord, we try to persuade others...]

We will be paid according to our works!

Do you know who needs to fear Gehenna?

[Luke 12:4-5: "I tell you, my friends [his disciples from verse 1], do not fear those who kill the body, and after that can do nothing more. But I will warn you [friends, disciples] whom to fear: fear him who, after he has killed, has authority to cast into hell [Gehenna]. Yes, I tell you, fear him!"]

He is not talking to enemies in this passage! He is talking to people who are in the family. "My friends." His disciples.

[John 15:13-15: No one has greater love than this, to lay down one's life for one's friends. You are my friends if you do what I command you. I do not call you servants any longer, because the servant does not know what the master is doing; but I have called

---

[76] 2 Corinthians 1:1 tells us that this is written to the church at Corinth, and as such, "we" refers to Paul, Timothy, and others who are faithful.

you friends, because I have made known to you everything that I have heard from my Father.][77]

The threat of Gehenna is to people who are in the family.

The lake of fire is literal. It is always used in a sense that is to be taken literally. Gehenna, however, is used in a figurative sense as a place of ruin. When you live a life of lawlessness, or even a life that is simply unprofitable, you will still be saved in the end, but your inheritance (your ***future*** salvation) will be ruined.

[James 3:6: And the tongue is a fire. The tongue is placed among our members as a world of iniquity; it stains the whole body, sets on fire the cycle of nature, and is itself set on fire by hell [Gehenna].]

Is your tongue literally burning? It may cause problems, but it is not on fire, although it sometimes should be. You may not mix and match metaphors. If your tongue is on fire figuratively, Gehenna is used figuratively.

More than that, Gehenna no longer exists.

[Jeremiah 7:30-34: For the people of Judah have done evil in my sight, says the LORD; they have set their abominations in the house that is called by my name, defiling it. And they go on building the high place of Topheth, which is in the valley of the son of Hinnom, to burn their sons and their daughters in the fire— which I did not command, nor did it come into my mind.

---

[77] It is interesting to note that although Jesus no longer calls them servants, Paul still calls himself a servant in Romans 1:1, Philippians 1:1, and Titus 1:1, James in James 1:1, Peter in 2 Peter 1:1, and Jude in Jude 1:1. Jesus also called many "brother", but nowhere does anyone call him brother.

Therefore, the days are surely coming, says the LORD, when it will no more be called Topheth, or the valley of the son of Hinnom, but the valley of Slaughter: for they will bury in Topheth until there is no more room. The corpses of this people will be food for the birds of the air, and for the animals of the earth; and no one will frighten them away. And I will bring to an end the sound of mirth and gladness, the voice of the bride and bridegroom in the cities of Judah and in the streets of Jerusalem; for the land shall become a waste.]

The name "Gehenna" itself come from the Hebrew "*geh*", which is "valley" and "*Hinnom*", which is a transliteration for the "son of Hinnom": *geh-ben-Hinnom*. "Hinnom" means lamentation, so it is the Valley of the Son of Lamentation. It is the Valley of the Son of Grief. It will one day be the Valley of Slaughter, "for they will bury" until it is full.

Those who lived there were sacrificing their children to Moloch, so the Lord told them to fill it up with dead carcasses.[78] If you go to Israel today and you look for that valley, you will not find it, because it is filled in. There is no longer an unquenched fire there. It was once a real place that is currently associated figuratively with judgment and ruin. It was a valley, in contrast to a mountain.

God judged Israel in Gehenna for their sins of idolatry and Jeremiah prophesied that the nation would be destroyed and their carcasses would be left in the valley as bird food. To quote Josey Wales, "Buzzards gotta eat same as the worms".

However, at the time Jesus was on the Earth, it was a literal place and fire was always burning there to burn the trash and keep

---

[78] The 180,000 man army of Senacharib, which the Lord slaughtered, is buried there, and that goes a long way toward beginning to fill it up.

things somewhat clean and sanitized. The dead bodies of criminals who were guilty of capital offenses would be thrown into the valley, and the constantly burning fire somewhat covered the stench.[79]

This gives us the context for Matthew 5:21-22.

[Matthew 5:21-22: "You have heard that it was said to those of ancient times, 'You shall not murder'; and 'whoever murders shall be liable to judgment.' But I say to you that if you are angry with a brother or sister, you will be liable to judgment; and if you insult [you empty, vain, worthless person] a brother or sister, you will be liable to the council; and if you say, 'You fool,' [you morally bankrupt person] you will be liable to the hell [Gehenna] of fire.]

If you are slandering a brother or sister in Christ, you are in danger of Gehenna. The brethren are those who are being obedient. Truth is not slander, but there are appropriate ways to correct a brother or sister.

"Sticks and stones may break my bones…" You probably should not hit a brother with sticks and stones either, but what does God say about words?

[Leviticus 19:16-18: You shall not go around as a slanderer among your people, and you shall not profit by the blood of your neighbor: I am the LORD. You shall not hate in your heart anyone of your kin; you shall reprove your neighbor, or you will incur guilt yourself. You shall not take vengeance or bear a grudge

---

[79] This is probably the reason Joseph of Arimathea fought so hard to get the body of Jesus; he wanted to prevent him from being thrown in with the criminals.

against any of your people, but you shall love your neighbor as yourself: I am the LORD.]

You can become a murderer by demonstrating hatred through slander.

[1 John 3:14-15: We know that we have passed from death to life because we love one another. Whoever does not love abides in death. All who hate a brother or sister are murderers, and you know that murderers do not have eternal [*aionian*] life abiding in them.]

Hate is found 32 times in the Bible. If we do not love, we hate. In the Bible, there is no middle ground! In Matthew 5:44, cursing is equated with hate. In Matthew 6:24, refusing to serve is hate. Matthew 10:23 we find that persecution is hate. Given up to affliction, betrayed and handed over (Matthew 24:9-10), separated, rejection of proper authority, not nourishing and cherishing, not ministering to brethren who are in need. There is love and there is hate. Period.

"Hate" is comparative, not an absolute. We are only given two words for comparison, "love" and "hate", so there are no other options for the words. No idea of malice is necessarily implied in the word. A good example showing that malice is not necessarily involved is in Romans 9:13 in which Jacob is loved and Esau is hated. Matthew 6:24 tells us we cannot serve two masters: We will hate one and love the other. We can love two masters (or Jacob can love two wives), but we will show preference to one. In Luke 14:26 in which we are told that if we do not hate mothers, fathers, siblings, spouses, and even our own lives, we cannot be disciples. We are obviously not supposed to go kill ourselves or our parents. Hate is a preference. Do these things come between you and God? Each of these things has a proper place and that place is represented by "love" and "hate".

The world hates the truth. We can be guilty of hate if we are angry for vain reasons. Haman hated Mordecai because Mordecai did not honor him. Saul hated David because David did better than Saul. We are given many examples.

If we want to enter in (enjoy our full allotment) to life, we must live by faith. We cannot be lawless and expect a reward. A murderer cannot live by faith. We can become murderers if we hate or slander a brother or sister in Christ. If you hate your brother, you will enter Gehenna and you will be ruined.

If you are an overcomer, you will not be hurt of the second death; if you are not an overcomer…

[Revelation 20:6: Blessed and holy are those who share [part or share] in the first resurrection.[80] Over these the second death has no power, but they will be priests of God and of Christ, and they will reign with him a thousand years.]

We need to fear the Lord. It does make a difference how we live our lives. We need to make sure we live our lives in such a way that our part or share is preserved. We need to be well pleasing to the Lord.

Do you want to hear, "Well done, good and faithful servant" or do you want to hear, "you wicked and slothful servant"? If we hear the latter, it will not be a pleasant experience.

---

[80] Not "first" as in numerical sequence, but "first" as in best quality. There are seven distinct resurrections spoken of in the Bible, and three of them are referred to as part of the "first" or better resurrection.

As a believer who has acknowledged that the Lord Jesus Christ died for your sins, your place in the family is secure, but your position within the family is not. There are many who correctly teach the security of the believer, but then fail to teach the accountability of the believer. They teach security as a license to sin. They teach that all sins – past, present, and future – are taken care of and it does not matter how you live. You get a clean slate and it stays that way.

[1 John 1:9: *If* we confess [present; durative action] our sins, he who is faithful and just will forgive us our sins [subjunctive; if we confess] and cleanse us from all unrighteousness.]

If we continually confess, he will forgive. If we do not continually confess our sins, he remains faithful and just, and that means our sins are not forgiven and we are not cleansed; we will be held accountable. We need to clean our slates on a daily basis. Most us need to clean our slates much more frequently than that.

If our sins – past, present, and future – are forgiven and forgotten, why do we need to confess them? Do we need cleansing and forgiving if they do not exist?

The penalty has been paid for all sins – past, present, and future – but we have to access that forgiveness and cleansing by confessing.

Why?

Because sin keeps us from having fellowship, and we need that fellowship because this is a team sport. If a player quits or becomes disqualified, it hurts the entire team. It is contagious.

We all need to be well pleasing to him because we will receive the things done in ***the*** body, whether good or bad. We will receive merit pay. You will get what is coming to you, and that can be either a threat or a promise.

[1 Corinthians 11:27-33: Whoever, therefore, eats the bread or drinks the cup of the Lord in an unworthy manner will be answerable for the body and blood of the Lord. Examine yourselves, and only then eat of the bread and drink of the cup. For all who eat and drink without discerning the body, eat and drink judgment against themselves. For this reason many of you are weak and ill, and some have died. But if we judged ourselves, we would not be judged. But when we are judged by the Lord, we are disciplined so that we may not be condemned along with the world. So then, my brothers and sisters, when you come together to eat, wait for one another.]

We are to tarry when we share in the commemoration of the Lord's Supper so we can judge ourselves today so we will not be judged in that day that is coming. How do we do that? 1 John 1:9: We confess our sins.

If we produce gold, silver, and precious stones, our works will survive the burning; if we produce wood, hay, and stubble, they will not survive. We can have treasure or we can have a pile of ashes, and it all depends on our works in the body, whether good or evil.

"Knowing the fear of the Lord, we persuade others…" (2 Corinthians 5:11) The context here is not persuading others to believe on the Lord Jesus so they can be born from above and saved spiritually, but persuading others to behave themselves the

156

way they ought to because their works will be judged. Those who are unsaved (not in the family; not born from above) will not be there. Knowing the fear of the Lord, we need to exhort others and warn them of the consequences of their behavior, so they can make changes before it is too late.

We're all in this together; keep your stick on the ice.

A portion of all proceeds goes to help ministries around the world.

Made in the USA
Columbia, SC
27 September 2022

67712894R00091